Elements in Early Christian Literature
edited by
Garrick V. Allen
University of Glasgow

LITERATE WORKERS AND THE PRODUCTION OF EARLY CHRISTIAN LITERATURE

Isaac T. Soon
University of British Columbia, Vancouver

CAMBRIDGE UNIVERSITY PRESS

Shaftesbury Road, Cambridge CB2 8EA, United Kingdom

One Liberty Plaza, 20th Floor, New York, NY 10006, USA

477 Williamstown Road, Port Melbourne, VIC 3207, Australia

314–321, 3rd Floor, Plot 3, Splendor Forum, Jasola District Centre, New Delhi – 110025, India

103 Penang Road, #05–06/07, Visioncrest Commercial, Singapore 238467

Cambridge University Press is part of Cambridge University Press & Assessment, a department of the University of Cambridge.

We share the University's mission to contribute to society through the pursuit of education, learning and research at the highest international levels of excellence.

www.cambridge.org
Information on this title: www.cambridge.org/9781009527217

DOI: 10.1017/9781009527224

© Isaac T. Soon 2025

This publication is in copyright. Subject to statutory exception and to the provisions of relevant collective licensing agreements, no reproduction of any part may take place without the written permission of Cambridge University Press & Assessment.

When citing this work, please include a reference to the DOI 10.1017/9781009527224

First published 2025

A catalogue record for this publication is available from the British Library

ISBN 978-1-009-52720-0 Hardback
ISBN 978-1-009-52721-7 Paperback
ISSN 2977-0327 (online)
ISSN 2977-0319 (print)

Cambridge University Press & Assessment has no responsibility for the persistence or accuracy of URLs for external or third-party internet websites referred to in this publication and does not guarantee that any content on such websites is, or will remain, accurate or appropriate.

For EU product safety concerns, contact us at Calle de José Abascal, 56, 1°, 28003 Madrid, Spain, or email eugpsr@cambridge.org

Literate Workers and the Production of Early Christian Literature

Elements in Early Christian Literature

DOI: 10.1017/9781009527224
First published online: November 2025

Isaac T. Soon
University of British Columbia, Vancouver
Author for correspondence: Isaac T. Soon, isaac.soon@ubc.ca

Abstract: This Element provides a historical overview of the sources and key scholarship related to literate workers in early Christianity. It argues that literate workers were indispensable for the creation, production, maintenance, interpretation, and preservation of ancient Christian thought, theology, and literature. This Element centers the embodiment and lived experience of literate workers – as much as is able to be retrieved from our extant Christian sources. Who were they? What did they look like? What was their relationship with named authors? What kinds of aspirations and career trajectories did they have? The aim of this Element is to help researchers reconfigure their perspectives on ancient works, that such documents represent the genius not only of named authors but also of (enslaved) literate workers as well.

Keywords: literate workers, secretary, enslavement, embodiment, Christianity

© Isaac T. Soon 2025

ISBNs: 9781009527200 (HB), 9781009527217 (PB), 9781009527224 (OC)
ISSNs: 2977-0327 (online), 2977-0319 (print)

Contents

	Introduction	1
1	Embodied Persons: The Bodies, Status, Gender, and Age of Literate Workers	8
2	The Mechanics of Use: The Materials, Education, and Practicalities of Ancient Literate Workers	17
3	Multipurpose Persons: Literate Workers as Translators, Interpreters, Emissaries, and Informants	29
4	Prosthetic Sons and Disabled Fathers: Disability, Augmentation, and the Christian Secretary	35
5	The Works of Us: Prolific Dictation and the Mirage of the Great Commentator	40
6	Pathway to the Episcopate: Secretarial Work as a Precursor to an Office	50
7	Invisibility, Critical Fabulation, and Recovering Literate Workers in Early Christian History	53
	Bibliography	65

Introduction

The literate worker in the ancient Mediterranean world is the ever-present author between the ancient sources that we know today and the figures whose names were appended to such works.[1] From the Roman politician Cicero to the natural historian Pliny, from ancient Greek cities to local villages in ancient Egypt, from Josephus and Philo to the high priest in Jerusalem, from the biographies of Jesus of Nazareth to the endless commentaries and treatises of writers such as Origen, Augustine, and Jerome, literate workers were present behind the scenes facilitating the formulation, composition, rewriting, and publication of ancient documents. Literate workers were present among ancient cultures of the ancient Mediterranean, and they continued to be present as the empire transitioned from Roman togas to Christian vestments.

This Element provides a historical overview of the sources and key scholarship related to literate workers in early Christianity. It argues that literate workers were indispensable for the creation, production, maintenance, interpretation, and preservation of ancient Christian thought, theology, and literature. Recent studies on literate workers in the ancient world focus largely on identifying their presence and uncovering their technological and social roles in the production of ancient documents. Current scholarship draws particularly on *critical fabulation*, an approach that uses the depiction of literate workers in the ancient Roman world as *comparanda* to reconstruct obscured lived experiences in the absence of explicit sources in our archive. This Element builds on this approach and attempts to reorient our understanding of extant Christian sources to retrieve and recover the present voices of literate workers.[2] Who were they? What did they look like? What was their relationship with named authors? What kinds of aspirations and career trajectories did they have? The aim of this project is to center the lives of literate workers and not treat them as "placeholders" (to use the *lingua* of Ellen Muehlberger),

---

[1] Readers should note that while I argue these literate workers are authors in their own right, that I use the term author sometimes in this Element as variant terminology for the person who dictates or on whose behalf literate workers write. This person is sometimes their employer or sometimes their master. It is important to emphasize, however, that while I argue that literate workers should be considered authors from our perspective, because of the very clear ontological distinction between enslaver and enslaved in the ancient world, ancient elite authors would not have viewed subordinates in the same standing. See Howley, "Despotics," 38. I am grateful to the two peer reviewers of this Element whose comments improved my overall argument.

[2] On this specifically see Section 7.

mere appendices or extensions of the authors with whom they worked.[3] The aim of this project is to help researchers reconfigure their perspectives on ancient works, that such documents represent the genius not only of named authors but also of (enslaved) literate workers.

How is such an endeavor possible? Though our sources may ultimately be aggregated by named-patristic authors, it remains the case that literate workers were involved in the shaping of their own depictions. In other words, our sources are amalgamations of perspectives, and the depiction of such workers is mediated through the work that they themselves have had a hand in creating. To use a musical analogy, texts generated by literate workers are like "chords." When we focus only on the tonic note (the named author, e.g., Jerome, Origen, and Paul) we are ignoring the harmonies (literate workers) that also contribute to the character of the chord as well.

One of the earliest studies on literate workers and the production of early Christian literature was a 1905 study by Erwin Preuschen who analyzed the well-known use of stenographers in the work of Origen of Alexandria.[4] Preuschen's focus is largely on how Origen's stenographic team enabled his wider ministerial exploits (e.g., combating heretics) and stresses that Origen was only able to author so many works because of these stenographers. Reflective of this early stage of scholarship on literate workers, Preuschen unsurprisingly focuses on Origen's own literary contributions over those of the stenographers themselves. For Preuschen, highlighting Origen's use of stenographers serves a larger text critical argument, that is, the development of initial Origene documents and the effect of literate workers on the felicity of transmission. When literate workers are mentioned, it is only in the context of the errors they might have introduced into the manuscript tradition.

Evariso Arns, in 1953, provided a comprehensive catalogue in Jerome's work of references to literary production paying attention to both the wider Greek and Roman literary context and the nomenclature used to describe different roles, materials, processes, and products.[5]

In 1978, Jürgen Scheele published a prodigious study of Augustine's use of literary forms, technology, and production.[6] The last section of his study focuses on Augustine's literary process, especially from dictation to reader. Scheele meticulously details Augustine's day-and-night use

---

[3] https://themarginaliareview.com/on-authors-fathers-and-holy-men-by-ellen-muehlberger/
[4] Preuschen, *"Die Stenographie im Leben des Origenes."*
[5] Arns, *La technique*. In 1957, Gert Kloeters wrote a dissertation on books and writing in Jerome, which is unfortunately inaccessible to me.
[6] Scheele, *Buch und Bibliothek*.

of literate workers to read works to himself. He even goes so far as to characterize Augustine's secretarial team "as collaborators in scholarly work" (sondern auch als Mitarbeiter bei der wissenschaftlichen Arbeit).[7] Thus, he argued that stenography was essential to the production of Augustine's body of work.

Another significant work in the study of literate workers in the production of early Christian literate was published by Thomas Graumann in 2021.[8] His book focuses on the production and use of oft-neglected early Christian documents, the ecclesiastical acta that recorded important discussions during conciliar proceedings and meetings. Such documents are important for understanding theological discussions that took place among early Christian communities as well as the social situations in which these discussions occurred. Graumann details everything from the kinds of documents used and how they are handled to the practicalities of stenographic dictation amid the furor of ecclesiastical debate. His work is a full-fledged expansion and improvement of the earlier work of H. C. Teitler on ecclesiastical notaries.[9]

Past scholarship in classics and early Christian history was focused on named Christian authors and their production of books. When literate workers were mentioned at all, it was usually with reference to nomenclature (*notarius*, *librarius*, etc.), the instruments and materials of production, or their typically rote service to authors like Jerome, Origen, or Augustine who then had to edit and smooth out the mistakes made by the literate workers. In New Testament specifically, previous scholarship focused literate workers ("scribes") in relation to textual criticism and the formation of autographs, initial texts, and manuscript copies of scriptural documents (which is not the focus of this Element).[10] An influential work that focused on the New Testament is E. Randolph Richard's 1991 book on ancient secretaries and the letters of Paul.[11] Richards provided an introduction to ancient secretaries in the Mediterranean world as well as a close analysis of the ways in which literate workers could shape the documents produced (e.g., style, content, and length). He argues that Paul's use of secretaries was probably largely editorial and had less to do with the shaping of the content itself.

---

[7] Ibid., 87.
[8] Graumann, *The Acts of the Early Church Councils*.
[9] Teitler, *Notarii and exceptores*.
[10] For a helpful overview of scholarship on scribal habits, book production, and textual criticism, see Haines-Eitzen, "The Social History."
[11] Richards, *The Secretary*.

At the turn of the millennium, initiated by the work of Kim Haines-Eitzen, the study of early Christian literate workers took a cultural turn, moving from the bookish and material focuses of past scholarship to the cultural and social aspects of literate workers. Haines-Eitzen's important work identified women literate workers in the production of early Christian literature. Her first book, published in 2000, argued for the importance of understanding the social contexts of ancient Christian scribes.[12] While she focused on the communal and paideutic contexts of these workers, the highlight of her work is her attention to the role of women scribes in the production of Christian documents. This latter study burgeoned in a second book, published in 2012, which analyzed the bookishness of Christian women as authors, producers, users, and collectors.[13] Although much of her work focuses on representations of elite Christian women and their involvement in literary production, her studies opened up the field to think about literate workers apart from scholarly issues of authenticity or text criticism.

The recent edited volume by Coogan, Moss, and Howley not only is an essential state-of-the-art resource for literate workers in the ancient world across classics, archaeology, and early Christian studies but also represents the maturation of the cultural turn initiated by Haines-Eitzen, with the desire to marry advances in book studies (especially the materialism of literature and its influence on the world) with cultural studies (e.g., enslavement, disability, power, and agency).[14]

Candida Moss's landmark 2024 book emerges out of this pursuit and focuses not only on the essential role that literate workers had in writing the New Testament but on the problematic contexts of enslavement that enabled its production.[15] Slavery is not only a central message within New Testament texts, but the New Testament itself is a product of enslavement. Moss's book – which is undergirded by vast swathes of contemporary scholarship on enslavement and literary production in classics and biblical studies – begins to recover the influence and agency of enslaved workers in the emergence of ancient Christianities.

Two final works are worth mentioning. Chance Bonar's 2025 monograph on God, enslavement, and early Christianity analyzes the figure of Hermas in the *Shepherd* in order to understand how early Christians conceptualized enslaved textual labor and deployed it in their own writings.[16]

---

[12] Haines-Eitzen, *Guardians*.
[13] Haines-Eitzen, *Palimpsests*.
[14] Coogan, Moss, and Howley, "Introduction," 1–2.
[15] Moss, *God's Ghostwriters*.
[16] Bonar, *God, Slavery, and Early Christianity*.

Finally, Ella Grunberger-Kirsh's recent rigorous work on the intricacies of learning stenography and the lived experiences of ancient stenographers examines not only the brutal lives of enslaved literate workers but also their contributions to shaping late antiquity, not least the Christian church.[17]

The approach of this Element – the centering and foregrounding of literate workers in the production of early Christian literature – is necessary for the larger discussion of the field in three ways. First, research on literate workers has focused largely on their role in the construction of the anthology of the New Testament. Rather I extend this discussion into snapshots of literate workers used by early Christian authors to generate other Christian literature such as letters, translations, commentaries, and ecclesial conciliar documentation (e.g., *acta*).[18] This Element shifts the focus away from a canonical emphasis to the realm of biblical receptions, *Wirkungsgeschichte* (working history) and early Christian culture. Second, this approach is necessary since it attempts to gather in one place (as much as is possible for a volume of this size) extant primary texts related to literate workers in early Christian literature. Certainly, there is more to be found than mentioned in these pages. The aim here is to be comprehensive but not exhaustive. Having an analysis of the sources in one place will be useful as a foundational reference tool for further research on this topic. Third, while current scholarship draws on pagan Graeco-Roman exemplars (e.g., Tiro and Cicero) with some reference to early Christian material (often, Origen in Eusebius/Jerome), this Element provides a broader range of early Christian exemplars that can extend and nuance already existing analyses of wider Mediterranean practices.

My project advances two modest interventions. The first is that the lived experiences and perspective of literate workers are recoverable (to a relative degree) from our ancient sources. The second, and more significant intervention, is that these depictions not only show their participation in the creation of early Christian literature, but they also show us glimpses of who they were, their aspirations, their personalities, their embodiments – who they were, what they looked like, where they lived, and who they became.

This Element will help students and scholars gain insight into the extent of which workers were involved in the creation of early Christian literature. It joins the growing chorus of scholarship that emphasizes such workers were not merely empty vessels but were rightful agents in themselves.

---

[17] Grunberger-Kirsh, *"The Memory Writers"*; "Etched."

[18] We do not discuss apocryphal narrative texts particularly because it is unclear whether they can be relied upon historically, see Teitler, *Notarii and exceptores*, 82–85.

I use the term "literate workers" as an umbrella designation to refer to literate professionals who were deployed (whether through enslavement or by hiring) in the production of some kind of ancient text. In scholarly translations and literature, there are many different types of nomenclature for these workers such as "secretary," "scribe," "clerk," or "stenographer."[19] In this study, the nature of our sources related to these literate workers is principally found in Greek and Latin literature, using terms such as γραμματεύς, ταχυγράφοι, βιβλιογράφοι, τοπογρ(αμματεύς), ὑπογραφεύς, *notarius*, *scriba*, and *ab epistulis*. Of course, none of these roles necessarily is wholly uniform from one context to the other. They can involve reading, transcription, dictation, forgery, diplomacy, archival work, and so on. The "text" generated can also be everything from an inventory list, expenditures, letter, gospel, commentary, council records, or heretical testimony. At the same time, however, all these positions involve some level of high literacy, writing, and production, which is the focus of this Element. Therefore, despite the variety of terminology, this Element uses "literate workers" to designate this class of workers, with terms such as "secretary," "scribe," "shorthand writer," or "amanuensis" used synonymously.[20]

Although the vast majority of ancient works that we have from history passed through their hands, we do not have an exhaustive historical or material record for literate workers in the ancient Mediterranean world that detail who they were. Subsequently, the paucity of evidence necessitates drawing on a wide pool of ancient evidence from Greek, Roman, Egyptian, Jewish, and early Christian sources from the second–third centuries BCE to late antiquity (up to and including the fifth–sixth centuries CE). Naturally, the portrayals in this Element are synthetic as I draw diachronically upon sources to provide analysis for instances of literate work in synchronic contexts. Readers should note that the selectivity of my portrayal is tempered by the limitations of our historical archive. Still, ample evidence from documentary papyri, iconography, and textual sources provides a coherent enough window into some of the ways that literate workers lived and worked.

---

[19] For the most recent up-to-date overview of the intellectual history and essential bibliography in both contemporary and ancient Mediterranean secretarial studies, see Moss, "The Secretary"; Grunberger-Kirsch, "Etched."

[20] This is not entirely alien to the ancient world. Basil of Caesarea for example describes "writers" as a larger umbrella class that could refer to calligraphers or stenographers. *Ep.* 134.1. For the complexity of classifying literate workers in the ancient world and the overlap between different nomenclature and the roles of literate work, see Teilter, *Notarii and exceptores*, 5, 29–31; Haines-Eitzen, *Guardians*, 21–35.

Readers should also note that the scholarship cited in this Element and in the bibliography is by no means exhaustive nor even comprehensive. The nature of the Elements series necessitates stringent selectivity. At the same time, the resources mentioned here are useful and fruitful starting places for graduate students and researchers studying this topic.

Section 1 explores the embodied realities of ancient literate workers in the wider Mediterranean, focusing specifically on physical appearance, disability, education, gender, and status. This section argues that while our historical archive is fragmented, it is historically plausible and likely that early Christians used both enslaved and formerly enslaved men and women in their literary endeavors. Section 2 explores the mechanics of using literature workers (secretaries, stenographers, copyists, readers) when producing early Christian texts (reading, writing, editing, rewriting) in its wider ancient Mediterranean context. Section 3 analyzes the multipurpose roles that literate workers occupied in everyday activities but primarily also in the context of early Christian councils. It focuses not only on the creation and administration of conciliar acts (minutes from previous meetings), but the translation, interpretation, and, in some cases, emissarial work that secretaries carried out within and without the walls of conciliar meetings. The section will focus also on the use of exchanged/borrowed literate workers as informants and spies.

Section 4 analyzes the frequent occurrences where literate workers are called upon to aid disabled authors (e.g., Jerome). While current scholarship views literate workers as, in part, forms of literary prosthetics, they can also be understood as augmentations. In other words, literate workers can be a prosthetic to offset physical impairment and disability, or they can be a corporeal augmentation for authors to extend their Self. Both configurations exist at the social, cultural, and physical expense of the worker.

Section 5 analyzes the creation of large bodies of Christian literature, especially multiple series of commentaries (e.g., Origen, Jerome), and how the production of this literature was contingent upon the use of literate workers. With a particular focus on their absence from the writing process and how it stifles production, this section will show just how dependent the creation of early Christian literature was upon literate workers. Many patristic fathers should primarily be understood as "dictators" and coeditors with their literate workers who serve as meaningful contributors to ideas and translation and therefore should be considered authors in their own right.

Section 6 analyzes the paths of three early Christian bishops (Eunomius of Cyzicus, Proclus of Constantinople, and Selinus of the Goths) who in our sources began their careers as (enslaved) literate workers in previous episcopates. It will highlight their historical situations, rise to power, and legacy amid critiques of heresy, sophistry, and barbarism.

Section 7 concludes by reflecting on the widespread characterization of literate workers as invisible and whether it is necessary, given the nature of the particularities of this historical archive, to draw *first* upon speculative methods like critical fabulation. It argues that the recent advances of early Christian scholars to solidify the involvement of enslaved literate workers as authors can be taken further. Drawing on the conclusions from previous sections, this final section suggests a few methodological advances to challenge presuppositions about scholarly conceptions of ancient invisibility and the historical archive concerning early Christian literate workers.

1 Embodied Persons: The Bodies, Status, Gender, and Age of Literate Workers

In discussions of literate workers, scholars often move swiftly into what these educated experts did rather than who they were. This section begins by thinking about the embodied information we can know about literate workers in the ancient Mediterranean past. The aim of this Element is not specifically only on the details of the mechanics of transmission (an emphasis of Section 3), which is already the focus of several classic studies and a growing field in early Christian studies. This Element concerns the embodiment of the literate workers themselves, as much as can be recovered.[21] Readers should note that our ancient evidence is partial and therefore the figures explored in this section are not representative of all literate workers but are merely instances that demonstrate the likely reality of some.

Generic features can be discerned from ancient iconography depicting literate workers. In almost all our depictions, literate workers are depicted as able-bodied men with the ability to stand, sit, walk, and hold items. They are usually clothed in robes; they have heads of hair sometimes curly and longer and other times shorter and cut tightly around the fringe of their forehead. In reliefs, few features are distinguishable or distinctive. But, in a mosaic from Thabraca for example (on the coast of modern-day Tunisia), a scribe's features reflect the slightly darker complexion common in mosaic images from north Africa.[22] It is important to note that

---

[21] This Element purposefully tries to think about individual literate workers as much as possible, but I acknowledge that they cannot be entirely separated from their wider scribal networks. On the latter, see Haines-Eitzen, *Guardians*, 77–104.

[22] For a more recent image, see the photo by Brent Nongbri, "A Mosaic from Thabraca." Now housed at the Bardo Museum in Tunis.

few, if any, of these examples are depicted as real historical individuals as opposed to general caricatures with relatively standardized and stock statuary characteristics. Even if they were based on someone who lived, given ancient artisanal technique in drawing from real-life features, we are not able to tie them to any one historical person.

There are at least two physical descriptions of literate workers in antiquity preserved in our sources. One concerns the ultra-Arian bishop Eunomius who was formerly a secretary. There are some small descriptions of his physical appearance preserved in Philostorgius but also in Rufinus of Aquileia. According to Photius's epitome of Philostorgius's work, Eunomius had "leprosy" and speech dysfluency:

> Philostorgius describes the appearance of his face and the rest of his features and likens to pearls the words from his mouth. Further one, however, he inadvertently acknowledges that he stammered, and does not to hesitate to glory his stutter as highly polished speech. He also maintains that the leprous patches that had disfigured and spotted his face had actually adorned his body.[23]

We are given two important pieces of information. One that Eunomius lived with speech dysfluency, a "stutter," but that he also lived with spots on his face and body that is described as "leprosy." It is impossible to diagnose specifically what Eunomius's condition might be – and it is certainly not related to what is now known as Hansen's disease – but it may be related to the contemporary condition vitiligo where the depigmentation of skin leaves spots of whitened skin (this is, as it so happens, similar but perhaps not exactly the same as ancient Jewish conceptions of *tza'arat* where skin whitening is sometimes a feature).

Given that we are dealing here a person that is condemned in Christian tradition as a heretic, how do we know that this description is historically accurate? In the ancient world where physiognomic interpretation was widespread, that is, the association between physical features of the body and moral character were intertwined with one another, it would be unsurprising to find an unfavorable physical description of a heretic. Rufinus of Aquileia mentions how Eunomius "was a man leprous in body and soul and outwardly afflicted with jaundice, but exceedingly able in debate; he wrote much against our faith and gave rules about debate to the members of his sect."[24] Here Rufinus reads Eunomius's physical appearance as a reflection of his polluted soul, though differently slightly in detail with

---

[23] Philostorgus, *Hist. eccl.* 10.6. Translation from Amidon, *Philstorgius*, 137–38.
[24] *Hist. eccl.* 10.26. Translation from Amidon, *Rufinus of Aquileia*, 419.

Philostorgius saying that Eunomius was "jaundice." Still, he acknowledges that Eunomius was a skilled debater and prolific writer, recognizing Eunomius's life-long dedication to oratorical writing. By describing the spots of his skin and particularly that his oratorical style was impaired, Philostorgius paints Eunomius as less than physically ideal. Despite what other readers viewed as physical shortcomings, Philostorgius does not view Eunomius negatively, but very much praises him.[25] While others like Rufinus used Eunomius's condition to portray him as physiognomically corrupt, Philostorgius, who was an admirer of Euonmius, would have had every reason to exclude details about Eunomius's speech ability and skin condition to bolster his portrayal. Yet he includes them. On this we may take such details as historically sound.

Another physical description of a literate worker that we have is from a letter written during from the early fifth century CE. Synesius of Cyrene was a bishop in Ptolemais (ancient Lybia) and wrote a letter describing a stenographer he met in Thrace.[26] Synesius asks a friend to track down a worker, whose name was Asterius, to give him a bedspread mat that the bishop had promised as a gift. Teitler is surprised that Synesius would stoop so low and go to such great extent for a lowly worker: "One wonders whether it was only a sense of guilt at having failed to fulfil his promise which prompted Synesius to write this letter. Could a *tachygraphos* have been so influential that he could not be disregarded with impunity?"[27] Synesius provides very specific locational and corroborative details about Asterius because there may be someone else in the city with the same name and profession (a possible hint at Asterius's enslavement). Synesius describes Asterius as "Syrian by race, black skin colour, slender-face, moderate in size" (Σύρος τὸ γένος, μέλας τὸ χρῶμα, τὸ πρόσωπον ἰσχνός, τὸ μέγεθος μέτριος).[28] Unlike the iconographic reliefs we have, Synesius provides us with a historically grounded description of Asterius, the literate worker, his face, his stature, his skin color, and his ethnicity. Not all

---

[25] Alana Nobbs argued that later writers such as Socrates, Sozomen, and Theodoret all wrote in response to Philostorgius' challengingly positive portrayal of Arian views in the fourth–fifth centuries. Nobbs, "An Alternative Ideology," 280.
[26] *Ep.* 61.1–5.
[27] Teitler, *Notarii and exceptores*, 76, Greek transliterated.
[28] Translation mine. For the critical edition, see Garzya and Roques, *Lettres I–LXIII*, 76–78. For the most recent English translation, see Fitzgerald, *The Letters of Synesius*. Fronto does mention a literate worker named Niger (Latin for "black") and this *may* be an indication of his enslaved status as well as his skin color, but we cannot say for sure. T 81 Fronto, *De feriis Alsiensibus*, Ep. 3.1.

workers shared these exact features, of course. But nevertheless, Asterius's description gives us insight into *one* worker's physical appearance.

It is not immediately clear whether Asterius is enslaved. On the one hand, Synesius describes him as being part of a "association" or "group" (συμμορία) of shorthand writers; at the time Synesius knew him the third or fourth, but perhaps now the first head writer (this suggests a company of at least five or more workers).[29] Participation in this group does not necessitate that he is simply employed, as we have evidence of ancient associations with mixed members where both enslaved and free persons were a part of the same group.[30] Additionally, as Vlassopoulos argues, Christian assemblies were, from early on, mixed associations in which men and women, enslaved and free(d) persons, and people from different ethnic backgrounds participated together.[31] It could very well be that Asterius's group is made up of mixed membership. On the other hand, the physical description of his features and the fact that Synesius has to distinguish him from others who might have the same name and profession tantalizingly resonate with descriptions of enslaved persons in ancient papyri.[32] Additionally it is suggestive that Synesius is wanting to give an Egyptian rug (δάπις) that Asterius can use as a mattress (στρωμνή). It is likely that Asterius did not have a mattress (a feature common among ancient slaves). This combined with Asterius's evolving living situation that makes him difficult to find suggests he was enslaved, since enslaved workers did not necessarily have dedicated or permanent residences.[33]

The status of secretaries in the ancient world did truly vary.[34] Some could be freeborn, others were formerly enslaved (freedmen) or enslaved themselves.[35] Furthermore, even if they were not always enslaved, as

---

[29] Compare Teitler, *Notarii and exceptores*, 76–77 who thinks that Asterius's guild is part of the *officium* of the *praefectus praetorio*.

[30] In ancient inscriptions from Italy, Greece, Macedonia, and Asia Minor from the first century BCE through to the fourth century CE we see mixed group assemblies well-represented: *IRhodPC* 21, *IG* V, 1 209, *CIL* VI 30983, *IEph* 2200A, *IGUR* 160, *IG* II^2 2361, *GRA* I 68, *GRA* I 72.

[31] Vlassopoulos, *Historicizing Ancient Slavery*, 144–45.

[32] For example, P. Cair. Zen. 59076 or UPZ 2 181.

[33] Whether Asterius is enslaved or not, there is the further important question of how a lack of dedicated living space or permanence might have affected workers like Asterius and their work.

[34] For some, secretarial work was the lowest form of enslaved labor (e.g., Seneca, *Ep.* 90.25, Kirsh, "Etched into the Soul," 62); however, for others, it was a higher form of labor (cf. Haines-Eitzen's analysis of P. Oxy. 3197, *Guardians*, 4).

[35] Teitler says, "On the notary, very often stenography was the work of slaves, or at any rate of *humilores*." *Notarii and exceptores*, 28.

Moss argues, they were nevertheless in a profession where they were still considered "servile."[36] The status of literate workers is not always mentioned in our ancient texts because it is not always relevant to the context or did not seem relevant to the ancient author writing about them. Recent scholarship, importantly stressing the enslaved status of this particular class of workers in the ancient world, largely characterizes these workers in the Roman Mediterranean as enslaved. But in early Christian sources, it is not always entirely clear if they are enslaved or not.

It is a well-established fact that ancient Christians, even into late antiquity, owned and used slaves. While a few ascetics appeared to abhor enslavement (e.g., Gregory of Nyssa, Naucratius, Macrina) the vast majority of Christians were comfortable owning slaves. This has moorings in New Testament texts where both Jesus and apostolic figures such as Paul and Peter endorsed systemic enslavement.[37] In the early second century CE, Pliny the Younger details his torturing of two enslaved women deacons.[38] Polycarp, the famous martyr, owned two slaves in his household.[39] The Acts of Andrew portrays the sexual use of slaves as surrogates for women who wanted to live ascetically and no longer have sexual relations with their husbands.[40] The Theodotian Code records Christian laws that restricted Jews from owning slaves who were Christians, but did not restrict Christians from owning slaves.[41] The principle was not the restriction of enslavement but that Christians could own slaves of other religions while Jews could not. Augustine argued for the essentiality of enslavement in God's divine order.[42] Even in the sixth-century CE Transjordan, wills from a Christian family in Petra reveal the division of enslaved workers named Salamanios and Almasia and Kyriakos and Ampelion (who themselves are descended from other household slaves, Ooue and Kyriake) among three sons.[43]

Although it is rarely clear whether the literate workers used by early Christians were enslaved or not, it is not the case that as time went on there was a greater likelihood that early Christians used hired secretaries rather than enslaved ones in the production and maintenance of their literary

---

[36] Moss, "Fashioning Mark," 195.
[37] Luke 12:41–48; 1 Cor 7:20–24; Col 3:22–25; Eph 6:3–9; 1 Pet 2:18–25; 1 Tim 6:1–2; Titus 2:9–10. See Charles, *Silencing*.
[38] *Ep.* 10.96.
[39] Mart. Pol. 6:1–2. Compare Ignatius, *Pol.* 4. See Shaner, *Enslaved*.
[40] Acts Andr. 14, 17 (cf. Tertullian, *Ux.* 2.8.4).
[41] For example, 16.9.1–2. Potentially stemming from Constantine (cf. Eusebius, *Vit. Const.* 4.27.1). See Glancy, *Slavery*.
[42] *Civ.* 19.15–16.
[43] P. Petra II 17, ll.64–66, 136–38.

endeavors. We have evidence of Christians using enslaved secretaries even at the end of the fourth century CE. In January 363 CE, in a letter to the Prefect of Egypt, Ecdicius, the emperor Julian wrote to acquire the library collection of the bishop of Alexandria, George, who had only a month before passed away.[44] Julian specifically asks the prefect to seek out George's secretary who can help track down all of George's books and that if he completes this task, he will gain his freedom. Another letter, *Ep.* 38 details instructions to a certain Porphyrius. There Julian mentions the torturing of other slaves in the household to track down all of the books. Here we have evidence not only of the bishop of Alexandria in the late fourth century owning slaves but that at least one of those slaves, one of potentially a whole group, was a literate worker.

With early Christian sources, I do not think we can presume in the absence of any particular clarifying details whether any given secretary was enslaved as a default although I acknowledge the high probability that the majority of workers mentioned in our texts were probably enslaved. At the same time, however, the opaque status of ancient literate workers – especially those working with early Christian authors, interpreters, councils, and so on – opens up the *possibility* that any literate work could have been created by enslaved workers. Despite the fact that we cannot verify with certainty enslaved participation in every early Christian document, we can acknowledge that enslaved workers played a pivotal role even beyond the first centuries in the creation and production of early Christian literature.

Our ancient Christian sources do not mention many explicit instances of women literate workers.[45] Eusebius says that some of the calligraphers who worked with Origen on his commentaries were women (see Section 5). Kim Haines-Eitzen also argues that Melania the Younger, Caesaria the Younger, and a certain "Thecla" named in traditions about Codex Alexandrinus also serve as evidence for literate Christian women workers.[46]

We do have broad Mediterranean evidence of women who worked as literate workers, largely from epigraphic sources. Cat Lambert bemoans the paucity of sources concerning women literary workers: "We hear about them, for the most part, after they have died, as etchings on

---

[44] *Ep.* 23.
[45] The dimorphic binary here is only presented because in our sources we have women and men labelled as literate workers. This does not preclude the historical reality of gender variation among secretarial workers in the ancient Mediterranean.
[46] Haines-Eitzen's, "Girls Trained in Beautiful Writing" reworked in *Guardians.* See also a certain "Grapte" in Herm. Vis. 2.4 whom Lambert argues may have been enslaved or formerly enslaved based on her name. Lambert, "Gender," 49, n.23.

stone."⁴⁷ Haines-Eitzen has highlighted the many extant inscriptions that mention women as readers, scribes, notaries, librarians, or copyists.⁴⁸ Two examples will suffice, one from Dio Cassius and the other from a second-century tombstone in Italy. Dio Cassius records the story of an enslaved concubine of the emperor Vespasian named Caenis who had an excellent memory and who was enslaved as a secretary for the mother of Claudius, Antonia.⁴⁹ Cassius highlights how her memory was so sharp that anything dictated to her could never be erased, a clear contrast to the erasable writing tools often employed by literate workers (see Section 2).

A second-century CE marble funerary relief now housed at the Staatliche Kunstsammlungen in Dresden depicts a Roman butcher shop.⁵⁰ The butcher stands chopping meat with various elements of a pig (head, ribs, innards, leg) hang overhead. Across the way a woman, presumably his wife, is seated writing on a set of multi-panel wax tablets. She is portrayed with fashionable robes and stylish braids. Given the depiction of clothing and the memorial on a monument of a small tomb somewhere in Rome it is unlikely that this woman was enslaved (or at least at the time of death she may not have been enslaved). Still, it is a witness to women literate workers in the second century. Recently analysis of the colophons of medieval and early modern manuscripts estimates that, conservatively, over 100,000 manuscripts were copied by women scribes with about 8,000 still extant.⁵¹ Given that women secretaries were known in the ancient world, it is therefore highly likely that there were a wide range of women literate workers deployed in ancient Christian context as well.

There were, of course, serious physical consequences for literate workers if they were enslaved in the service of their masters or employed by other households. Corporal punishment, beatings, and torture were all potential possibilities and realities in both Christian and non-Christian contexts. There was even potential for sexual violence. We get a glimpse of the sexualization of literate workers in Martial's figurative depictions of slaves as *libelli*.⁵² Talitha Kearey notes, "Martial, both poet and pimp, offers his libellus a choice between two types of forced sex work."⁵³ While

---

⁴⁷ Lambert, "Gender," 49.
⁴⁸ CIL, 6.3979, 7373, 8786, 8882, 9301, 9525, 9541, 9542, 33982, 33473, 34270, 37802.
⁴⁹ *Hist. rom.* 65.14.1–2.
⁵⁰ Inv. Hm 418. An image is accessible here: https://skd-online-collection.skd.museum/Details/Index/166524.
⁵¹ Ommundsen, Conti, Haaland, and Holst, "How many medieval and early modern manuscripts were copied by female scribes?"
⁵² e.g., Martial, *Ep.* 1.3.1–3, 9–12; 3.2.
⁵³ Kearey, "Editing," 198.

Christian sentiments about the temperance and moderation of masters might present theological ideals, the varied and sobering reality was likely very different in the everyday. We are not able to retrodiagnose the precise kinds of psychological conditions such workers might have faced as a result of their enslavement, but we do know from contemporary research that corporal and sexual violence causes mental-health-induced trauma, with conditions like post-traumatic stress disorder (PTSD).

Although we are not able to diagnose the mental health conditions of ancient literary workers we are able to say something about the physical and disabling toll that scribal activity had on their bodies. Recent research focusing on osteoarcheological analysis of ancient Egyptian scribes (from the third millennium BCE) indicate that scribal posture (cross-legged sitting and/or kneeling) in addition to writing increased the likelihood of osteoarthritis and strain from joints in the jaw, neck, shoulder through to the hands, legs, and feet.[54] Despite multiple millennia these Egyptian remains and early Christian scribes, shared practices (e.g., sitting cross-legged or in smaller spaces with legs confined) and long periods of strained writing meant that early Christian literate workers also faced similar disabilities and bodily transformations.[55]

The use of various document technology could also impact the bodies of literate workers. Candida Moss argues that "the constant winding and unwinding of a book roll would have damaged the carpometacarpal joint at the base of the thumb, producing arthritis, tendonitis, and other joint-related injuries."[56] She does, however, observe that the rise of the codex among early Christians may have positively impacted the physical labor involved in literate work or at least reduced the kind of strain exacerbated by earlier book technology.[57]

There is little firm information that we can know about the ages of literate workers in the past. Often when age is mentioned, it refers to the youthfulness of a secretary.[58] Candida Moss summarizes:

> Enslaved children could become accomplished copyists and even accountants at a prodigiously young age. By prepubescence, once basic literacy and numerical skills were acquired, they might move

---

[54] Havelková et al., "Ancient Egyptian scribes." See also Moss, *God's Ghostwriters*, 29–31.
[55] For visual examples, see the second–fifth-century CE relief at the Archaeological Museum of Ostia (Ostia Antiquarium, inv. 130). An image can be seen at Nongbri, "A Relief from Ostia."
[56] Moss, "Disability," 66.
[57] Moss, "Disability," 69–70.
[58] This is even the case in some of our epigraphic evidence from ancient Jewish contexts, where children as young as six and seven are noted. On this and the evidence see Schams, *Jewish Scribes in the Second-Temple Period*, 236.

on to apprenticeships to learn specialized skills like accounting or shorthand. A mid-second-century funerary inscription from the Roman port of Ostio attests to the skills of Melior, a thirteen-year-old boy who served as a bookkeeper for a prominent local administrator. That so many deceased children, both boys and girls, were buried with writing tools – pens, inkwells, and numerical counters for performing calculation – suggests that Melior was exceptional but not unique.[59]

The Roman poet Ausonius addresses his stenographer as "boy" (*puer*) that could be an indication of the youthfulness of his stenographer's age though it could possibly be a diminutive of affection.[60] Jerome mentions Paul a young man from Concordia in Italy who now had grown old but who had once been the secretary of Cyprian of Carthage.[61] Sometimes the youthfulness of a secretary is mentioned as a counterpart to their developing secretarial skills since youthfulness could be synonymous with problematically slow notetaking.[62] Occasionally, we do sometimes get a glimpse of their actual historical ages. Augustine for example in a letter describes a youth, a son of an elder named Armenus of Melonita, who served as his clerk having had experience as a stenographer at the time.[63] Augustine remembers him as a skilled stenographer who died when he was only twenty-two. Of course, the Christian writers who mention their literate workers often contrast them with their own elderly age and so every literate worker they encounter is likely some kind of "youth."

Materially, the earliest depiction of crucifixion, the so-called Alexamenos *graffito*, is simultaneously a witness to early Christian literate workers in the imperial household. The *graffito*, found in a possible paedegogium near the palatinate in second-/third-century CE Rome, depicts an enslaved youth honoring a man crucified on the cross with the head of a donkey. The accompanying inscription says: "Alexamenos worships God." In the history of interpretation, this image has usually been understood to be a non-Christian mockery of a Christian worker, one of our earliest if not the earliest visual example of anti-Christian rhetoric. More recently I have argued that it is possible that the graffito is not a depiction of a fellow Christian enslaved literate worker but could be a self-parody generated *by* a young ancient Christian literate worker.[64] Not all literate workers were young, of course,

---

[59] Moss, *God's Ghostwriters*, 26–27.
[60] Ausonius, *Ephemeris* 7.
[61] *Vir. ill.* 53.
[62] Rufinus, *Orig. Hom. Num.*
[63] *Ep.* 158.1
[64] Soon, "The Alexamenos *Graffito.*"

but when age does appear, it is their youthfulness that is often important. Youthfulness often (though not always) accompanies ability, and this will be a key part of understanding the way that early Christian authors used literate workers as prostheses for physical disability in Section 4.

2 The Mechanics of Use: The Materials, Education, and Practicalities of Ancient Literate Workers

Literate workers, specifically "scribes" (γραμματεύς), are mentioned frequently in the texts that are later assembled in the anthology known as the New Testament, particularly concentrated in early Christian gospel literature. Sometimes these workers are synonymous with other kinds of legal experts (e.g., lawyers and Pharisees) but we are given no insight into their everyday practices or function as portrayed in ancient Judea. There is also the further question of whether the authors of the gospels have depicted accurately these literate works in the first place. In other words, claims about the wholesale historicity of these texts are frequently doubted in relation to information about the historical Jesus of Nazareth; how much more for the scribal workers who are only peripherally deployed in the narratives. Candida Moss has argued that authors such as the apostles Paul and Peter used enslave literate workers in the production of their literature. Paul employed Tertius ("third"), an enslaved or formerly enslaved literate worker, to help him write his letters.[65] Peter's interpreter, Mark, whom Christian tradition says authored the Gospel of Mark may have been an enslaved secretary.[66] Ekaputra Tupamahu has cleverly argued that the "servants" mentioned in Luke 1:1–4 may refer to enslaved literate workers.[67] Chance Bonar argues that Sosthenes, one of Paul's coauthors in his letters, "was an enslaved or formerly enslaved literate worker."[68] Still, the information about literate workers in the New Testament is limited. Rather than drawing information about how literate workers were used from New Testament texts, scholars turn primarily to comparative conceptions in Greek and Roman sources.

Dio Chrysostom's advice was that rhetors should not write with their own hand but should prefer giving dictation into another's hands.[69] This

---

[65] Rom 16:22. For a discussion of Paul's possible vision loss and the use of secretaries and our understanding of Pauline pseudepigraphy, see Moss, "The Secretary," 23–28 and Moss, "What Large Letters."
[66] Moss, "Fashioning Mark."
[67] Tupamahu, "Language," 80–82.
[68] Bonar, *The Author*, 19.
[69] *Dic. exercit.* 18.

serves both a stylistic purpose and a practical purpose. On the one hand, less labor is involved for the orator. On the other hand, the thoughts that are written have the style of speech as opposed to written work. It should be noted, however, that this comment occurs specifically in the context of ancient oratory. As Nick Elder argues in his work on the production of gospel media, "For Dio in this passage, dictation is preferable not in and of itself, but for training in public eloquence....dictation is recommended for a particular purpose and kind of text."[70]

The first-century CE Roman biographer Cornelius Nepos argued that there was a distinction between Greek and Roman conceptions of secretaries.[71] He argued that scribes were merely hired workers since that is their role whereas in Greece the position of secretary was acceptable only for those who already come from both a highly respected family and displays superior ability.

One of the most famous examples of secretarial use in ancient Roman culture comes from Pliny the Younger's letters where he describes both his own practices as well as the practices of his uncle, Pliny the Elder. For the Younger, during the summer, from the moment the window shutters are opened and light is let in, his secretary comes and receives Pliny's dictation, a process repeated multiple times in a day.[72] His uncle on the other hand had a secretary permanently with him at all times with a book for reading and a notebook for notes.[73] The authorial relationship between the secretary and the person on whose behalf they wrote was often portrayed as one characterized by literary intimacy. Not in a romantic sense but in the sense that there was an expectation that secretaries speak with the same mind and verbal style as the named persons for whom they wrote.[74] We will explore this in further detail in Sections 4 and 5 where we think about literate workers as prosthetic extensions of their employer's bodies and as authorial voices in the works that they create.

The use of literate workers, enslaved or otherwise, in ancient Jewish contexts is more complex. Unlike Greek or Roman or early Christian authors, ancient Jewish literate workers were often, though not always, portrayed as being the authors themselves even though it is clear for scholars like Carol Bakhos that professional scribes were employed from the Second Temple period onward (especially in the transmission

---

[70] Elder, *Gospel Media*, 162.
[71] *Eum.* 18.4–5.
[72] *Ep.* 9.36.3.
[73] *Ep.* 3.5.14–15.
[74] Philostratus, *Vit. soph.* 2.94 (628).

of scriptural texts, for example, as demonstrated by the scrolls collected from the Judean desert).[75] This is not to say that ancient Jews in the Mediterranean did not employ literate workers at all but rather that the evidence of their individual use is very sparse, especially in the Second Temple Jewish period and in the literature of the rabbis in late antiquity.

Flavius Josephus mentions the use of literate workers in an ancient Judean context. For example, he describes a secretary, named Diophantus, who worked for King Herod and was an expert at forging the handwriting of others until he was put to death for forgery.[76] Outside of a royal context, Josephus also mentions a scribe who worked for the captain of the temple, a man named Eleazar (son of Ananias).[77] Christine Schams argues that this scribe "may have been the private secretary of Eleazar with possible responsibilities like the writing of correspondences, documents and maybe lists and records."[78] When retelling Jewish history Josephus also retrojects Roman literary workers (e.g., scribes) into biblical contexts.[79]

In the rabbis we find far less explicit evidence for the use of secretarial workers, though this does not mean that they were not used. Hayim Lapin argues that while rabbis themselves may have been literate they would have also drawn from wider skilled workers locally.[80] Carol Bakhos argues that "rabbinic literature attests to the notion that the copying of texts was considered a mere technical skill, from which rabbis distinguished their own more creative intellectual ability."[81] The Mishnah describes the presence of two scribes at the Sanhedrin, one standing on the left and the other on the right recording the arguments of the defense and the prosecution.[82] Schams notes that "the rule that two or three scribes should be present seems to be based on theoretical considerations of how to exclude mistakes in a courtcase."[83] Indeed, as we will see in Section 3, this is precisely the same late antique mechanism we see occur in some early Christian conciliar gatherings. In the Jerusalem Talmud we do have an instance where at the Temple Rabban Gamliel (roughly the 30s CE) asked

---

[75] On this see Bakhos, "Orality and Writing," 488–89.
[76] *BJ.* 1.529. Hezser, *Jewish Literacy*, 262.
[77] *Ant.* 20.208.
[78] Schams, *Jewish Scribes in the Second-Temple Period*, 137.
[79] For example, *Ant.* 11.244–68. On this see Schams, *Jewish Scribes in the Second-Temple Period*, 133–40.
[80] Lapin, *Rabbis as Romans*, 69.
[81] Bakhos, "Orality and Writing," 489; Heszer, *Jewish Literacy*, 467–75.
[82] m. Sanh. 4.3.
[83] Schams, *Jewish Scribes in the Second-Temple Period*, 227.

Yochanan the scribe (סופר יוחנן) to take down dictation.[84] The inscriptional record also shows numerous synagogues that had scribal workers as well.[85]

No study concerning wider Roman or early Christian literate workers has yet seriously engaged with ancient Jewish sources. For some reason, Jewish material has been segmented off from wider Mediterranean studies on literate work as though Jewish literary culture was cut off and uninfluenced by Roman scribal practices, even while evidence from Josephus (as noted above) indicates that Jewish writers knew and understood literate work in Roman ways. This is unfortunate in particular because we do have extant autographic letters made by literate workers. I speak here of the Bar Kokhba letters, a series of correspondences in Aramaic and Greek from the second century CE.[86] These epistolary autographs contain important clues about the use of literate workers in Judea during this period, practices that may be helpful in thinking comparatively with wider Roman and later Christian material. For example, P. Yadin 54 is sent by the a scribe named Shemuel son of Ammi.[87] We know that it is written in his hand since the name and the script are written with the same hand.[88] There is also P. Yadin 63 which mentions the sending of a letter written by the hand of Shimon son of Yishmael.[89] Finally, and most interestingly, there is P. Yadin 52 which is a letter written in Greek where the sender, a Nabatean named Soumaios, has been forced to write in Greek because whoever is scribing (whether he or someone else) is not able to write in Hebrew letters.[90] This tells us more than just the kind of variety of literacy among figures involved in the Bar Kokhba revolt; with literate intermediaries in mind it tells us that Soumaios does not have a literate work available to write in Hebrew lettering (so perhaps only trained in one or two languages) but that the recipient, Yonathes son of Beianos, may have a literate worker who can read both Aramaic and Greek. Some scholars like Michael Owen Wise argue that some of the letters may have been rough drafts initially composed by a secretary, such as P. Yadin 49.[91]

---

[84] b. Sanh. 11b.
[85] For the epigraphic sources consult Schams, *Jewish Scribes in the Second-Temple Period*, 235–38.
[86] For texts and translations see eds. Yadin, Greenfield, Yardeni, and Levine, *Documents from the Bar Kokhba Period*.
[87] Column II, l. 17.
[88] Greenfield, Yardeni, and Levine, *Documents from the Bar Kokhba Period*, 359.
[89] ll. 4–6.
[90] For detailed notes, see Greenfield, Yardeni, and Levine, *Documents from the Bar Kokhba Period*, 357–60.
[91] Wise, *Language and Literacy in Roman Judea*, 223.

Integrating sources concerning literate workers in an ancient Jewish context is an important path forward in understanding early Christian uses of literate workers.

Across cultures, literate workers were not necessarily employed in a uniform framework all of the time. The piecemeal nature of our evidence, often coming from elite contents and rarely from only the workers themselves, means that the reconstructions of their use, including the one in this section here, should not be taken as paradigmatic but illustrative. Workers could be employed by individuals, public and private, elite and imperial, but also collectively to be shared in a particular household. The Emperor Julian wrote about how all the secretaries in his household were occupied and so he had to write a letter himself.[92] This suggests a collective of literate workers were shared among his household.[93]

There is a frequent motif in our ancient sources, Christian and pagan, that emphasizes the "at hand" nature of secretaries.[94] In Section 5 we will discuss the absence of these workers, how it can affect the construction of a text, and the extent to which for some early Christian authors depended on these workers for the completion of their texts. For now, I emphasize the expectation they are largely present wherever their employers or masters are. They often emerge out of the shadows when suddenly there is the need for someone to take town an immediate dictation. A modern analogy might be the pulling out of a smart phone to take a voice note or to write down an idea in a notes app. Similarly, although they only emerge narratively when authors incorporate them into their writings (and there is something strangely meta about secretaries describing their own presence in the writing), we should presume their constant presence. Sarah Blake notes how the Latin term *manus* in relation to enslaved workers elicited four conceptual categories, that slaves were physically proximate and legally owned by their masters, they were proficient instruments for masters to use, and they were literary proxies.[95] It was a ubiquitous practice that literate workers were expected to be available at all times with varying

---

[92] *Ep.* 9.

[93] Likewise, papyri attest to village-secretaryship (κωμογραμματεῖαι) of a certain Menches in Kerkeosiris (Egyptian Fayum) that did not only include administrative literary duties but also cultivation of land. *P. Tebt.* 10.

[94] For example, Pliny the Younger, *Ep.* 9.36.3, 3.5.14–15; Marcus Aurelius to Fronto, Ad M. Caes. v. 26; T 81 Fronto, *De feriis Alsiensibus, Ep.* 3.1; Lactantius, *Mort.* 46; Origen, *Comm. Jo.* 6.2.9.; Ausonius, *Ephemeris* 7; Julian, *Ep.* 9; Basil of Caesarea, *Ep.* 134.1; Sidonius, *Ep.* 5.12. Even in ancient iconography do we see the scribe standing proximate to their dictators.

[95] Blake, "In Manus," 89.

degrees of spatial proximity and accessibility awaiting the moment of their simultaneous objectification and textualization as they are drawn out of the narrative silence to inscribe the voices of their masters.

The primary function of ancient literary workers was unsurprisingly bibliographic, which included reading literature, managing and repairing documents, taking dictation, note-taking, and finalizing drafts.[96] There was no singular way that literate workers were used.[97] Ancient literate workers were charged a variety of different literary tasks. One of the most basic uses of literate workers in the ancient world was to have them read aloud works at all times of day and in all places.[98] Principle among them was reading literature for their clients (even sometimes reading in other languages).[99] Paul of Concordia, the secretary for Cyprian of Carthage, used to read the works of Tertullian to him daily.[100] Augustine talked about a young secretary who used to spend every evening reading to him.[101] Sometimes stenographers were even employed to take down public discourses. For example, Eusebius describes Origen in his elderly age (60 years old) allowing his public lectures to be written down, something Origen that apparently never before permitted.[102]

Secretaries were also responsible for various kinds of bookkeeping, such as transporting books and making them available even if their master was on holidays or cataloguing their libraries.[103] Bookkeeping did not just also imply transporting and maintenance of books but also storage of important documents. Cicero mentions secretarial practices of compiling decrees.[104] Libanius mentions an enslaved secretary who would store letters in case he needed to use them to his advantage in the future.[105] This was a practice regularly done by secretaries. As Alexandra Leewon Schultz notes, archives both personal and public were continually maintained by literate workers.[106] In later Christian sources, we see instances where copies of now lost or misplaced documents had to be retrieved from

---

[96] On the maintenance of ancient books under Roman rule, see Nongbri, "Maintenance."
[97] Different scholars have given broad overviews of processes using literary workers, for example, Howley, "In Ancient Rome," 22.
[98] Sometimes given the label *lectores*, but as with all nomenclature, it was not necessarily specific to those who were given this title. Horsfall, "Rome without Spectacles," 49, 54.
[99] Compare P. Yadin 52 above.
[100] Jerome, *Vir. Ill.* 53.
[101] *Ep.* 158.2.
[102] Eusebius, *Hist. eccl.* 6.36.1.
[103] Cicero, *Fam.* 16.20; T 81 Fronto, *De feriis Alsiensibus*, Ep. 3.1.
[104] *Dom.* 129.
[105] Libanius, *Or.* 1.177 (F 165).
[106] Schultz, "Collection," 207.

the scribes who had originally wrote them.[107] Important documents and correspondences were copied multiple times with one being sent off to the recipient and the other being placed for safekeeping in case the "sent" correspondence was lost (much like a carbon copy). This might explain one reason why multiple literate workers might be present at any given time apart from function (e.g., secretary, stenography, and calligrapher) or circumstance (e.g., in case multiple copies need to be sent to multiple recipients at the same time).[108] Multiple copies could be produced concurrently.

The ability of stenographers to capture the very thoughts of their dictators in the wax tablets of their work was viewed with astonishment, and some ancient authors alluded to this skill as prescient (see Section 5).[109] Since literary workers were praised for their memory (e.g., Caenis) and knew intimately the patterns of thoughts, linguistic/stylistic/cheirographic tendencies of their masters, this combination of skills supplied the right conditions for forgery, especially of letters.[110]

The close proximity of secretaries to the authors with whom they worked can be demonstrated by the fact that sometimes when literate workers died, their masters needed consolation. Libanius in the fourth-century CE talks about how the applause from an oration he had given had comforted him in the death of the secretary who helped him revise his notes.[111] Augustine speaks affectionately about his young secretary who used to read passages multiple times and enquire of the bishop what something meant.[112] This constant proximity made Augustine call him a close "friend."

Literate workers were not only used for the composition of original works. Their remit also concerned translation and annotation.[113] An interesting example is seen a letter from Jerome who details a letter sent by Pope Epiphanius that had caused a stir in Palestine. There were few copies, but many wanted to read. A local man, Eusebius of Cremona, begs Jerome to translate the letter from Greek into Latin. Jerome does so with the use of a secretary who wrote down Jerome's dictated version of the letter on the side margins on of several chapters of the letter itself.[114]

---

[107] Synseius, *Ep.* 67.34.
[108] For the latter, see Lactatnius, *Mort.* 46.
[109] For ancient sources, pagan and Christian related to dictation, see Norden, *Die antike Kuntsprosa*, 953–59.
[110] For example, Cicero, *Dom.* 129; Josephus, *BJ.* 1.529; Sidonius, *Ep.* 1.7.5.
[111] *Or.* 1.232 (R 142).
[112] *Ep.* 158.2.
[113] On this see Sections 3 and 5.
[114] *Epist.* 57.2. It is fascinating that Jerome calls this a "translation" even though it began as notes in the side margin of the original text.

Myles McDonnell reminds us that it was a cultural trope that elite members would write things (e.g., personal letters) by hand and even sometimes correct works that they had written themselves and not necessarily outsource it all to an enslaved literate class.[115] As Moss argues, writing down dictation via longhand was of course an option, albeit slow since it involved syllable by syllable (and potentially letter by letter! Depending on the skill of the literate worker, cf. Herm. Vis. 2.1.4) dictation.[116] The vast amount of work, however, went to enslaved literate workers. The quality of work done by literate workers is only infrequently mentioned, most often not when it is positive but when the workers are too slow. Chance Bonar argues that complaining about the poor ability of literate workers was an occasional Roman practice in our sources.[117]

Some ancient secretaries were skilled in stenography or shorthand, being able to write quickly using abbreviated signs and then finishing and revising the draft of the work after dictation has concluded.[118] For example, Marcus Tullius Tiro, Cicero's secretary, famously was said to not only have received dictation from Cicero but also to have invented the *notae Tironianae* shorthand.[119] One oft-cited source for the amount of time it took to learn shorthand is P. Oxy. 4.724 where Panechotes, an official from the second century, sent away his slave Chaerammon at great expensive to learn shorthand. Chaerammon was to study for *at least* two years in a house full of other learners until he had fully learned the entire stenographic handbook known as the *Commentary*.[120] The instilling of the symbols and ideology on stenographic workers led some like Basil of Ancyra to say "If someone stripped away (a stenographer's) fleshly body, they would see every inch of his soul scrawled over with the *Commentary* carved into it."[121]

For stenographers who wrote dictated notes in shorthand, there was the expectation that they fully expand the notes later on.[122] The specialized nature of stenographic signs meant that, as Moss argues, short hand writers "were not interchangeable fungible workers; they were an inextricable

---

[115] On this see McDonnell, "Writing, Copying and Autograph Manuscripts," esp. 477.
[116] Moss, "The Secretary," 46.
[117] Bonar, "Notes," 95.
[118] Ausonius, *Ephemeris* 7.
[119] *Qint. fratr.* 3.1.19. The latter point inferred from Plutarch, *Cato Min.* 23. On Tiro and related scholarship, see Tempest, "Tiro." Aulus Gellius famous leveled many critiques about the work of Cicero's longtime stenographer, Tiro. On this see Howley, *Intellectual Narratives*, 192–213. I cite Howley's dissertation since this section was not included in the published monograph. Howley, *Aulus Gellius*.
[120] Grunberger-Kirsh, "Etched into the Soul," 62.
[121] Translation from Grunberger-Kirsh, "Etched into the Soul," 63.
[122] Ausonius, *Ephemeris* 7.

part of the writing process without whom the text was unreadable."[123] Additionally, sometimes masters would compose and compile their own notes and then a secretary would revise and clarify notes for ease of use later on.[124] They would also proof read and interpret their master's handwriting when copyists were not able to decipher their particular ligatures.[125] Sometimes after the deaths of their masters, they would publish their notes in edited collections.[126]

What might the process of literary production look like? This would have been different from case to case given the nature of the work, the number of literate workers involved, and the types of literate workers present (e.g., stenographers, secretaries, calligraphers, copyists). Multiple people could have occupied the same "position" (e.g., stenographers and secretaries). One way of thinking about this – and this is not completely represented in any one source but is discernable based on the nature of the kinds of literate workers we find in our ancient Christian sources – is to think of a simple progress of stages. A secretary would be asked to retrieve books, the materials would be read (perhaps by the named author or perhaps by the secretary), the named author will dictate, the stenographer takes down the notes in shorthand, the notes are revised and/or turned into longer form notes, and corrections are made along the way. Once a polished draft is complete a calligrapher or copyist might make a polished draft for sending out to feedback among friends.[127] Further, revision would occur, and more copies made.

Another kind of literary process we see in our ancient sources when resources allowed is a "revolving door" policy. We see this in the construction of the works of Origen. The grandeur and extensiveness of Origen's work required near constant composition, and Origen describes the use of his secretaries who take breaks and "tag in" when one becomes fatigued. When the one working becomes fatigued another takes its place. In this way, all are used for a period of time, and all are able to take breaks to rest. Given the physical and mental strain of this kind of work, this use of literate workers allows for some temporary reprieve while allowing for continuous dictation and perhaps maximizing the longevity of workers.

---

[123] Moss, "The Secretary," 49.
[124] For example, Libanius, *Or.* 1.232 (R 142).
[125] For example, Cicero, *Fam.* 16.22.
[126] As attested about Tiro in authors like Aulus Gellius, *Noct. Att.* 1.7.1; 15.6.2; Quintilian, *Inst.* 6.3.4–5.; 10.7.30–31.
[127] On the publication of works and the dissemination process around a close inner circle of friends before more wide circulation see Starr, "The Circulation of Literary Texts"; McDonnell, "Writing, Copying, and Autograph Manuscripts," 486.

The technology most associated with ancient literate workers from are writing tablets (*tabula cerata* or *cera*) with a stylus.[128] These stylus tablets were made with wood (though sometimes other substances like ivory) with a recesses that enabled a wax surface. Users would use a stylus (e.g., made of metal) to inscribe marks upon the tablet. Users could re-flatten the wax using a spatula to "erase" or "refresh" the surface to then write again; they were reusable. Hundreds of the remains of these wax tablets have been found places such as Vindolanda, London, Pompeii, and Herculaneum, while a few have been found elsewhere such as Switzerland, Romania, and Albania. According to Roger Tomlin's analysis, the vast majority of those found in London, for example, were made from silver fir, a few from spruce and larch, and even fewer from maple.[129] Silver fir does not occur natively in Britain, primarily being concentrated in areas of what is now southern France, southern Germany, Poland, and Slavic nations. This suggests that they were imported to England, and it is likely that they were repurposed from cask timber.[130] While this is idiosyncratic to this particular region, it gives us an idea of how some ancient tablets were manufactured. Although the wax was meant to be refreshed sometimes users who were too vigorous would accidentally score the back of the wooden tablet and repeated use and repeated scoring preserve illegible fragmented details of the texts once written in the wax.

Multiple tablets couple be tied together (diptychs) or hinged with multiple tablets (triptychs, etc.). Typically, holes (two to four) would be drilled on the inside border of tablets and then the tablets were tied together. The image of the woman scribe at the butcher shop mentioned in Section 1, for example, depicts a set of multiple wax tablets sewn together. A painting on the upper south wall of the tablinum of the House of Giulia Felice (Inv. 8598) at Pompeii depicts a set of multiple wax tablets bound together along with a stylus as well as a single wax tablet on its own.

Literate workers used all kinds of different technology such as scrolls, wooden tablets, ostracon, papyri, parchment, and codices.[131] A codex, which would become the primary literary medium in late antique Christianity, possibly gets its name meaning "block of wood" because "in a Roman context the codex was made up of several wood tablets bound together."[132]

---

[128] Sidonius, *Ep.* 5.12. For other types of accessories, see Moss, *God's Ghostwriters*, 45.
[129] Tomlin, *Roman*, 6.
[130] For the manufacture of these particular tablets see Tomlin, *Roman*, 9–15.
[131] On overall book roll production, writing format, paratextual features, and diacritical marks, see Johnson, *Readers and Reading Cultures*, 18–22.
[132] Meyer, "Roman Tabulae," 300.

The physical posture of literate workers took multiple forms depending on the task and the literature they were producing, but Skeat's classic depiction is representative:

> Normally he [the scribe] sat crossed-legged, with his short kilt tightly stretched between his thighs, which thus formed a sort of substitute for a table or writing-desk on which the option section of the roll of papyrus law. While the right hand wrote, the left steadied the unwritten and still rolled-up portion of the roll, and unwound it as necessary. Other representations show a different posture, in which one knee was raised in front of the writer to form a sloping support for the open section of the roll, which then rested on the knee and thigh.[133]

Although Skeat had argued that "there is virtually no evidence for the use of chairs, tables or desks" in the production of ancient literature, recent work by Brent Nongbri on ancient iconographic and architectural remains shows that desk use before the fourth century is highly likely.[134]

In the ancient world, literate workers were not trained in any kind of uniform way. As Candida Moss argues, they could be educated at "urban 'slave schools' or alongside freeborn children in the household."[135] Eunomius, a bishop and later a condemned heretic according to our traditions, is said to have taught himself shorthand, not a small feat in itself.[136] Literate workers could also have been completely uneducated, like the way Hermas is portrayed in Herm. Vis. 2.1.4, copying a text out letter by letter because he could not copy the syllables.[137]

Sometimes the training received by literate workers was done by named authors themselves. Basil of Caesarea, for example, talks about calligraphers and stenographers that he himself has trained.[138] Some, potentially like Alexamenos, were trained to be literate workers from a young age. Others, however, might have changed careers and becoming secretaries or stenographers at a later period of time. A few of our early

---

[133] Skeat, "The Use of Dictation in Ancient Book Production," 7.

[134] Skeat, "Early Christian Book-Production," 58. For the preliminary findings of Nongbri who is currently preparing this material for publication see, "A Relief from Ostia," "A Relief from Portus," "A mosaic from Thabraca," and "The so-called Scriptorium." For a classic study on desks as a late rather than earlier development, see Metzger, *Historical and Literary Studies*, 123–37.

[135] Moss, "The Secretary," 40–41.

[136] On this see Section 6.

[137] Chance Bonar argues that Hermas's ability in this text may be less about his mere ability and more about God giving him the ability to understand written revelation. Bonar, "Notes," 96; Bonar, *Enslaved*, 127.

[138] *Ep.* 134.1.

Christian authors mention their literate workers who have gone back to a former way of life before they were scribal workers.[139]

While some workers may have been employed on their own – for example, if they were a personal secretary – we sometimes see collectives of literate workers employed as a team or working in a guild of professionals. Asterius, who we met in Section 1, was part of an association of writers possibly more than five or six. Synesius's description of the association illumines the way such workers were ranked, with each worker ranked in order from the first.[140] We do not know specifically what criteria were used to rank these workers. However, given Synesius's comment about Asterius becoming the first after being third or fourth previously, it may be that such workers were ranked in order of seniority.

Employment prospects for literate workers were not limited to individual or imperial households. They could be teachers, work as village or community scribes, work with book sellers, or private tutors.[141] As we will see in Section 6, literate work in close association with an episcopal master also opened up opportunities for ecclesiastical progression, from deaconships to elderships to bishopric positions although we should be cautious that this necessarily reflects kind of "upward mobility" that leaves behind servility of literate work.

For those secretaries who were paid for their work and not enslaved we cannot speak precisely about their remuneration across the Mediterranean since amounts would differ from place to place and project to project. There are occasions in early Christian literature where calculations must be made to see if there is enough money to pay for the completion of a work.[142] We do have occasional documentary evidence, however, which does point to remuneration, but it is not clear what particular services were rendered. So, in a papyrus (dated to 215 CE) documenting the monthly account of a temple of Jupiter Capitolinus at Arsinoe (at the northern point of the Red Sea), we find the monthly salary of Boethus, a scribe with a monthly salary of 40 drachmae.[143] Dioclesian's famous edict on maximum prices (301 CE) does attempt to place a cap on copyists at 20–25 denarii per 100 lines, depending on the quality of writing, but there is little evidence that this was actually followed. Proximity to elite figures often had economic benefits for literate workers. Suetonius mentions

---

[139] For example, Basil of Caesarea, *Ep.* 134.1.
[140] *Ep.* 61.4.
[141] Moss, "The Secretary," 41.
[142] For example, Origen, *Comm. Jo.* 6.2.6.
[143] B.G.U. 362, cols. 6–8, l. 14.

the emperor Claudius's secretary, Narcissus to whom the emperor was devoted and gave many financial gifts.[144] In the sixth century, Gregory the Great notes how Companianus, a senior military commander, had left twelve *solidi* per annum to his secretary.[145]

Even though not every literate worker was employed in the exact same way with the exact same set of experiences, from our ancient Mediterranean sources, we are able to understand the broad strokes of their labor and the physical realities of their day to day existence. The function of literate workers, however, was not confined only to books.

3 Multipurpose Persons: Literate Workers as Translators, Interpreters, Emissaries, and Informants

In the last section, I focused on many of the common daily uses of literate workers in the ancient Mediterranean world across Jewish, Greek, Roman, and early Christian cultures. In this section we will zero in on some of the particular Christian uses of literate workers we see in our ancient Christian evidence. These are not entirely unique to Christianity. Focusing on them, however, helps us to see some of the particular nuances related to secretarial use in Christian contexts, while also providing a useful set of comparison for wider Greek and Roman practices in the ancient Mediterranean.

One way that early Christian literate workers were used was as emissaries.[146] In the wider Mediterranean, literate workers delivered important documents to or negotiating between multiple parties.[147] They served advisory roles mediating and sometimes deciding between different courses of action.[148] Sozomen, the fifth-century lawyer and ecclesial historian, wrote about Marianus, a stenographer for emperor Constantine, who had delivered a letter to the bishops in Tyre to unify themselves so that they could dedicate the newly constructed "temple" at Golgotha (what is now the Church of the Holy Sepulchre).[149] Here we see Marianus function as an ancient letter carrier traveling far to deliver the emperor's letter. The work of Peter Head has highlighted how letter carriers in the ancient world were not merely postal workers delivering artefacts from one hand to another.[150] Some carriers, not least figures like Marianus who was in close

---

[144] For example, *Claud.* 28.
[145] *Regist.* 1.44.
[146] For example, Pseudo-Martyrius, *Orat. funeb.* 108.
[147] Cicero, *Fam.* 16.4; 16.17. Pseudo-Lucian, *Nero* 9. Amm. Marc. 26.5.14, 28.2.5.
[148] The sources are many. For example, Amm. Marc. 20.4.11, Ausonius, *Ephemeris* 7.
[149] Sozomen, *Hist. eccl.* 2.26.
[150] Head, "Named Letter-Carriers."

proximity to the emperor, would have been expected to supplement the written message with other oral reports from the sender. This means that for those literate workers who also acted as emissaries, their roles were not simply to transmit messages but to interpret, clarify, and supplement that information provided.

As noted in Section 2, one illicit use of literate workers was to generate forgeries, especially epistolary ones. In the case of suspected forgery, literate workers were summoned as witnesses as to the authenticity of written materials. In the fourth century, Athanasius of Alexandria was embroiled in a controversy where he was accused of writing letters to the tyrant Flavius Magnetinus who murdered Constantius II's brother, Constans.[151] Writing to Constantius II to clear his name, he interrogates the whole process by which these so-called letters have been used as evidence and provides evidence that refutes their authenticity and affirms his innocence in the matter. Athanasius argues first that even if they can produce these letters that the handwriting in itself proves nothing for certain. The handwriting would have to first be certified by his usual amanuensis to certify that it does indeed come from him. This is not because the secretary is most familiar with Athansius's hand but because the amanuensis will be able to recognize his own handwriting. A literate worker served as a witness for forgery, verifying or refuting based on their own personal knowledge of the literary hand in which documents were written.

It was not only in the calligraphic style of the document that a literate worker served as a witness for but also for the physical exchange of documents itself. Athanasius talks about how he has his writers and Magnetinus has his own servants who would have received letters from those who send them and give them directly to Magnetinus. Athanasius offers his own literate workers to testify about whether such epistolary exchanges ever happened, and he asks Constanius to summon the servants of Magnetinus who are probably still living. Here the literate workers on both sides of an exchange testified to whether the two had a literary relationship and did in fact know each other at all.

Literate workers were not only used to record and keep records of discussions with accused heretics but were also used as witnesses against their masters. In a highly polemical letter against his Arian replacement for six years (339–345 CE), Gregory of Cappadocia, Athanasius claims that his secretary, Ammon, proved Gregory's Arianness.[152] Christian literate

---
[151] Athanasius, *Apol. Const.* 11.
[152] *Ep. encycl.* 7.

workers were not only responsible for generating the work at hand but were responsible for their social afterlife, regarding their authenticity or felicity. Literate workers were therefore vital for the verification of authorial works since they were living witnesses of whether named authors did indeed have a hand in producing them.

Becoming informants against their masters proved personally problematic. Sulpitius Severus, a Christian scholar from fourth–fifth-century Gaul, complains about how his mother-in-law, Bassula, steals all of the things that he has written. In one of his letters, he speaks about how no piece of writing in his home, no book, no letter, or correspondence is sacred; everything that he writes, intended for public or private makes its way into Bassula's hand.[153] Sulpitius suspects that his secretaries are to blame, that they are likely informing and passing on what Sulpitius has been writing on to Bassula, potentially because she pays them (he speaks of her generosity toward them); for this reason, Sulpitious cannot blame them. Since she provides their wages, they are really *her* secretaries. Because of them, unpolished and unedited work find their way to the public without Sulpitius's consent.

This situation gives us insight into the dangers of shared literate workers and particularly their allegiances to those who employ them. Literate workers were not just vessels whose minds remained empty as dictation was given to them nor did they remain unchanged in the editorial and publication process. As in the example of Caenis mentioned previously, *they have memories*. Workers were thus deeply acquainted with the innermost thoughts, ideas, aspirations, and secrets of the masters or employers with whom they closely worked. In one sense, their greatest asset was also their greatest liability, and given particular kinds of relationships, the abilities of literate workers were taken advantage of. It is unclear whether Sulpitius is truly cross with his mother-in-law or if the letter is written in a kind of tongue-in-cheek way. Given a more hostile situation, however, were someone to access one's literate workers, perhaps bribing them through payment or gift or manumission, one would have access to a treasure-trove of information useful for extortion. Indeed, as we saw with Ammon above, the knowledge of a secretary could be used to anathematize a religious and political opponent.

One of the key ways that literate workers were used in an early Christian context is during bishopric synods, councils, or disputes, especially amid discussions of orthodoxy and heterodoxy (or heresy) and the sanctioning

---

[153] *Ep.* 3.

of those supporters of the latter.[154] The presence of literate workers at ecumenical councils and meetings is unsurprising since the recitation of texts, books, the taking of notes, and the recapitulation of previous notes was essential to the function of these gatherings. Records of councils in acts form a kind of ancient minutes that walk through who said what and actions taken at the time. As Thomas Graumann argues, although literate workers are not always explicitly mentioned in the records themselves, we know that they were undoubtedly present.[155]

In some of these, however, we get a glimpse into the participation of literate works, like at Chalcedon secretaries like a certain Constantine and Veronicianus read aloud materials relevant to the current discussion.[156] Ella Grunberger-Kirsh argues that Christian stenographers would have had to develop shorthand signs, "unofficial" symbols to meet the theological and doctrinal discussions being undertaken in these councils.[157] These shorthand signs were necessary simply because of the possible speed with which interactions took place.

As we saw in the previous section, literate workers could also assist with translating texts from language to another. Jerome's mentions "his" translation of a letter from Pope Epiphanius from Greek into Latin was produced with the help of a secretary.[158] In this instance, it is ambiguous how much Jerome and the secretary are contributing to the translation. Is it merely Jerome translation while the secretary writes or is the secretary doing the primary initial translation while Jerome checks it over? It might be a collaborative process where they each translate sections and correct element of it together.[159] We do have another example of a secretary translating a text, from Latin into Greek, unaided. In sessions from the council of Chalcedon, Veronicianus translates sections of texts for the bishops during the council.[160] Price does note, however, that sometimes Veronicianus's translations are "shockingly bad."[161] Regardless of one

---

[154] I acknowledge that this terminology is strongly weighted toward one way of viewing early Christian diversity. I use it in order to reproduce the framework used by the authors I deal with here while recognizing that the nomenclature is reductive and simplistic.
[155] Graumann, *The Acts of the Early Church Councils*, 114.
[156] Constantine: CChal. 4.2, 24; 14.14; 15.5; 16.16, passim. Veronicianus: CCahl. 1.48, 50, 51, passim.
[157] Grunberger-Kirsh, "Etched into the Soul," 77.
[158] *Ep.* 57.2.
[159] For more a more detailed explanation of the extent to which Jerome's literate workers participated in his translation, see Section 5. For a material example of secretarial correction, see Moss, "Between the Lines."
[160] Council of Chalcedon, Session 4. CChal. 4.50; 7.6.
[161] Price, *The Acts of the Council of Chalcedon*, 248 n. 11.

individual's perceived ability, such secretaries would be expected to work in multiple languages at a conciliar level.

Eusebius mentions a fascinating case where a principal of a school of sophistry in Antioch who was also a presbyter, Malchion, drew out the leader of a heresy, Paul of Samosata, resulting in the latter's excommunication from the church.[162] Malchion had a discussion with this heretical leader that Eusebius notes was strategically taken down and recorded by stenographers. Through this, Eusebius says, Malchion was able to deduce that this man had been fracturing the community and deceiving other believers. Eusebius even claims that the record of this discussion is still extant. It is unclear whether this interrogation took place publicly in the context of the synod where ecclesial secretaries would have been present or privately in the presence of other literate workers. Eusebius stresses that it was only Malchion alone who had the rhetorical skill through which to entrap Paul. In any case, here we find the use of a stenographer to record, not a letter or a sermon or a commentary, but a conversation between two people. The stenographers' notes would have been expanded into a widely readable format and then distributed by the bishops (or if it was conducted in the presence of the bishops, drawn upon for their final verdict of excommunication). As Graumann argues, such notes were "not just a background operation but an integral part of the council's formal business, because their notes entered the protocols as substitutes for the live voices of the absentees."[163]

Conversations concerning objects to heresy were not limited to public proceedings but sometimes also to private conversations among bishops themselves. Basil of Caesarea in a letter against his mentor and friend Eustathius of Sebasteia recounts on one occasion how several stenographers were present during a conversation they had together while the latter's disciples were present where Basil was refuting heresy.[164] Basil appeals to this instance to demonstrate that certain theological accusations against him are baseless since Eustathius has records of their conversations and that they would show Basil's innocence on the matter. These further stresses how theological views, especially those expressed within private conversations, if written down were vital pieces of evidence to acquit or condemn heretics. The work of literate workers was vital to the anti-heretical projects since it provided, in some cases, the only verifiable

---

[162] Eusebius, *Hist. eccl.* 7.29.1–2.
[163] Graumann, *The Acts of the Early Church Councils*, 115–16.
[164] *Ep.* 223.5.

evidence that some officials could use to condemn and excommunicate the messages of heterodox leaders.

During the council of Sirmium (351 CE), some parts of the debates between then-bishop Photinus and Basil of Ancyra were taken down by the stenographers who were present.[165] Epiphanius's account of this event tells us about the diversity of ecclesial literate workers who might have been present at a council involving heresy. Later, Sozomen, affirms that the discussion between Basil and Photinus was immediately taken down by stenographers.[166] In his record, Epiphanius notes five stenographers who were present. One was Basil of Ancyra's own deacon, Anysius, another was the governor Rufinus's secretary, Callicrates, others named Olympius, Nicetes, and Basil, and two imperial notaries Eutyches and Theodulus.[167] Epiphanius notes that three copies were made, one was sent to the emperor, Constantius II, another was kept by the council of Basil of Ancyra and another was sealed and left with court officials. Epiphanius's account apparently draws directly on these council records.

Why so many different types from different parties? Having a multiplicity of literate workers there from different parties allows for a level of objectivity regarding the things that were said. Verdicts about excommunication depended on the notes of these meetings to be used as evidence. Willful manipulation not only endangered the reputation of literate workers but also their lives as they could be criminally charged.[168] Should only one party have secretaries taking notes then there is an increased opportunity that notes might be altered or changed in order to support the case of one particular party. When one had literate workers from multiple parties, especially if works were going to be published or archived in a singular copy, then it served as a point of validation for the statements recorded therein. As Graumann notes about a different ecclesial gathering in Carthage, the presence of literate workers from two or multiple parties was "of fundamental importance" for avoiding "any impression of undue bias."[169]

In early Christianity, literate workers were involved not only in the private lives of authors but also in the public life of the Christian community. Since Christian writers depended on these workers so intensely at both a personal and communal level, in some cases they became extensions of named authors not just in terms of physical ability but also the authorial Self.

---

[165] Epiphanius, *Pan.* 3.71.1.6–8.
[166] Sozomen, *Hist. eccl.* 4.6.15.
[167] *Pan.* 3.71.8.
[168] Graumann, *The Acts of the Early Church*, 116.
[169] Graumann, *The Acts of the Early Church*, 117.

4 Prosthetic Sons and Disabled Fathers: Disability, Augmentation, and the Christian Secretary

The level that even nondisabled people (or people who are not explicitly associated with any impairment or disability) relied upon secretaries for their writing cannot be understated. Cicero speaks affectionately about the absence of his ill-secretary Tiro and how *their* work grinded to a halt given his absence.[170] Cicero claims he is not even able to read something to Pompey without Tiro. Julian writing in the winter of 361 CE mentions how he writes to his uncle late in the evening, but all the other secretaries are occupied and therefore he has "with difficulty" wrote the letter up by his own hand.[171] Even an emperor like Julian, who was literate and learned and had studied in Alexandria, was still greatly dependent upon literate workers to generate documents.

As mentioned in Section 1, the physical toll that literate work took on the body was more than aches and pains. It could result in lifelong impairment and disability, changing the very shape and structure and function of workers' bodies. This was recognized even in some of our ancient early Christian sources. Basil of Caesarea mentions in a letter to Paeonius that the total number of his scribes has dwindled in number, with some whom he trained going back to a previous industry or trade while others have abandoned their literate work altogether because they have become chronically disabled (ἀρρώστιες).[172] It was not just the immediate work itself that caused these physical issues but the *chronic use* of workers as extensions of masters' or employers' bodies that exacerbated physical impairments.

Secretaries and stenographers and scribes were social extensions of the bodies of those on whose behalf they wrote, whether they were employer or master.[173] The author speaks and the secretary writes; they are from, one point of view, a kind of literary technology, a human proxy for the author's own hands and writing ability. This is what Brendon Reay has termed "masterly extensibility."[174] This relationship is sometimes portrayed as a labor-saving relationship (so Dio Chrysostom), the secretary making the generating of documents easier on bodies. One common

---

[170] *Fam.* 16.10.
[171] Julian, *Ep.* 9.
[172] *Ep.* 134.1.
[173] For authors of early Christian scriptural texts, Paul is the mostly obvious candidate for this use since it may be the fact that he lived in some kind of visual impairment. On this, see Moss, "What Large Letters." On Paul's disabilities more broadly, see Soon, *A Disabled Apostle.*
[174] Reay, "Agriculture."

way of thinking about the relationship between authors and literate workers among our sources is through the metaphor of prosthesis. As Joseph Howley puts it, "In ancient Rome, reading was as often as not something you did with someone else's body."[175] Sarah Blake argues, "Slaves, when present, are envisioned as seamlessly fused prosthetic limbs acting together with their own instruments and with the master."[176] But we should be cautious, as Candida Moss argues, since the reduction of a person to a body part is a form of "psychic violence that dehumanized and degraded human beings."[177] The reducing of literate workers to limbs manifested what Jeremiah Coogan helpfully points out is the Roman inertia toward fragmentation: "The systems of distributed cognition in which Roman reading and writing were embedded existed not only to manage information that was 'too much to know' but precisely insofar as they facilitate expansive and exploitative projects of knowledge-making."[178] In other words the distribution of labor across multiple persons was not a way to equally share the burden of work, but was a way of taking advantage of the enslaved literate worker's body for the benefit of their enslaver.

At the same time, while we might think of this relationship as a social prosthesis – a cultural practice where literate workers are human augmentations to the persons of their dictators – we can also think about these workers as prostheses for disabilities with which ancient authors lived. In the second century CE, Marcus Fronto, for example, uses a secretary to give corrections on a speech that has been sent to him.[179] Fronto states that he has to use a secretary because his hand has been disabled by debilitating pain, pain affecting his body greatly that he has to be carried to the games. So, in this instance not only is the secretary a social prosthesis but an actual prosthesis enabling Fronto to write because his own pain prevents him from doing so.

Only a few of our early Christian writers mention the use of secretaries in the context of disability. The most prominent example is that of Jerome who lives with a number of conditions.[180] In the preface to his commentary on Galatians, Jerome speaks explicitly about how his fading eyesight and bodily infirmity prohibit him from being able to write with his own hand.[181] In his preface to his translation of the books of Solomon, he notes how this

---

[175] Howley, "Reading in Ancient Rome," 22.
[176] Blake, "Now You See Them," 207.
[177] Moss, "Disability," 64.
[178] Coogan, "Notes," 161.
[179] *Ad Amicos*, ii. 3 (Naber p. 191).
[180] On how Jerome's physical impairments affect the composition of his work, see Section 5.
[181] Prologue to book 3 of *Comm. Gal.*

condition has been chronic.[182] Because of this he relies on literate workers whose eyesight he exploits. In a letter completed overnight by lamp-light Jerome argues unlike other places where he finds himself ill that in this instance, he was speaking so swiftly that it was not even able to be taken down by shorthand.[183] In an age where accessible lighting to ease reading is so quotidian as to be invisible, it is easy to take for granted how in the ancient world the very architecture of a reading space would have to take into account when the best amount of light would be available for its users. As Horsfall notes, "Vitruvius is well aware of the ideal orientation for a private library. Very nice, if you had one, if your architect had remembered that morning light was best, if your heaviest intellectual commitments did not occur during the winter, when Roman hours of daylight are very short, and if you were free to write and read mostly in your own library!"[184] In the dark of winter, when oil lamps might be lit in the dim shadows of a workspace, when Jerome had his slaves read and write on behalf of him, it was *their* eyes not Jerome's that would face the physiological effects of eyestrain and *ophthalmia*. Jerome offset his own impaired eyesight by straining theirs.

Despite his prodigious output, Jerome deplores his own rhetorical ability. He calls it "slowness of utterance" but here it is not talking about an impairment, *per se*, but his own ability to revise a work. It is important to note that it is not simply that Jerome lacks the will or desire to revise his work, he states that he simply cannot do it. It might be the case that his physical disabilities, his eyesight and general bodily ability, exacerbate the work, so further revision (inducing pain) is neither feasible nor possible. In his preface to the third volume of his commentary on Amos, which he addresses to Pammachius (406 CE), Jerome explains how during his exposition of Hosea, Joel, and Amos he fell gravely ill.[185] This illness seems to be directly a result of the swiftness with which he began dictating again. While we have recognized that their work can greatly affect the health of literate workers, Jerome claims that dictation done too vigorously and hastily can have adverse health effects on the use of literate workers as well. In Jerome's case, he finds that his incessant work and recent return to commenting on Hosea, Joel, and Amos caused him to become ill in the first place.

---

[182] Preface to the Books of Solomon.
[183] *Ep.* 117.12. Augustine also mentions "two holy brothers" he is working with are too slow to receive his dictation. Augustine, *Ep.* 27.3 (Divjak letters).
[184] Horsfall, "Rome without Spectacles," 50.
[185] Preface book 3 of his *Comm. Am.* Also mentioned in the preface for his *Comm. Eccl.*

Because of both Jerome's inability to write and his ongoing illness due to the creation of these commentary works, Jerome's secretary is a literal prosthesis. It is not merely a *social* prosthesis, a kind of delegation of work that could be completed by a named author himself (albeit to an inferior degree of quality, in Jerome's mind). Rather, it is a prosthesis that *enables* Jerome to complete work that he physically would not be able to do on his own. The literate worker is a human augmentation, a skilled extension of Jerome's body. Cat Lambert argues that Romans like Seneca discouraged writers from exerting too much strain on their bodies lest their own physiology begins to mimic the emasculating positions of enslaved literate workers.[186] By augmenting themselves with enslaved workers, authors like Jerome, who lived with chronic pain, could retain what was left of their own bodily autonomy and masculinity.

Not all prostheses or augmentations were used to the same extent. Some literate workers were used in intentionally restrictive ways. This is the case with Jerome. As mentioned earlier, Jerome lives with compounding physical conditions. One was the inability to write with his own hand (at least to the standard that perhaps he expects of a literate worker). Another was the physical toll that dictation took on his body. The interplay between his physical conditions and the literary expectation of polished work causes Jerome to (claim to) limit the functionality of his secretaries.

Jerome contrasts two kinds of writers, those who write slowly and then later spend a large amount of time correcting their work, and others like him who employ secretaries and write quickly. When using literate workers to write commentaries on scriptures, Jerome claims that his aim is not oratorical and rhetorical flare, but rather simplicity and veracity of the message itself. Thus, unlike the writer who writes slowly and revises, Jerome, through a secretary, writes quickly and does not revise.[187] At the same time, Jerome's emphasis on his lack of revision may serve as a rhetorical ploy to offset his disability and show that the first thoughts that come out of his mind are as oratorically erudite as those revised by others with their secretarial workers.

Jerome is fully aware of how frustrating this must be for his literate worker. While his secretary says nothing, their body betrays the internal

---

[186] Lambert, "Gender," 46.

[187] He notes that sometimes when he is trying to complete a work quickly (e.g., a letter) he can bypass the need for rhetorical flare, not necessarily because of ability, but because of time constraints. It is not always clear what Jerome means by "revision." But we do know that even though he considers his work to be generally plainer, involving much less rhetorical elevation, he does acknowledge that in his other works he often weaves quotations from the scriptures into his writings. *Ep.* 117.12.

exasperation: a furrowed brow and clenched fists.[188] The literate worker's expectation is that they are there to help and improve the piece. Jerome not having the ability to revise, and – in the case of writing commentaries – not thinking it appropriate to make commentaries rhetorically stylish, refuses this help. Though the literate worker enables Jerome to write, Jerome nevertheless restricts the function of the literate worker. While they might *transcribe*, there is no correction or polishing. Jerome, in a way, then retains some of his own agency in this literary process, at least for rhetorical purposes; he is the one in control of the style of the writing, while his literate worker functions *merely* as a skilled hand.

The unification of prosthesis and author can be demonstrated by the importance placed upon matching a document's written voice with the person on whose behalf it was written. When there was disjunction between what was written and the expected literary style, the secretary was not doing their job properly. So, Philostratus, writing in the third century CE, writes about a certain Aspasius of Ravenna who became the imperial secretary but wrote letters on behalf of the emperor in an inappropriate unclear style (e.g., the use of enthymemes).[189] For Philostratus this is tied to the function of law; what is written must be crystal clear because what the emperor says becomes law.

As a literary prosthetic, because workers functionally aided authors, if their own bodies became dysfunctional then their *raison d'être* could be put in jeopardy. They required the ability to hear, to see materials and their master's face, to be able to write, and so on. If their bodies ceased functioning, then they would need to be replaced. For example, a literate worker who did not have pristine hearing during a church council could be a secretarial liability as sessions involved tremendous noise. Thomas Graumann notes, in such environments there was continuous shouting, interruption, and private conversations, sometimes from opposite sides of the room; all things difficult for someone without a hearing impediment, even more so for a literate worker whose hearing began to deteriorate.[190] There is also the earlier well-known example of Zosimus and Encolpius both who become ill from overrecitation to Pliny.[191] Pliny waxes poetic about their unfortunate physical conditions but it is clear that his "servile apparatus" has malfunctioned. Although the two of them have become

---

[188] Preface to book 3 of *Comm. Gal.*
[189] *Vit. soph.* 2.94 (628).
[190] On noise and the sonic spatiality of councils, see Graumann, *The Acts of the Early Church Councils*, 128–29, 170.
[191] Blake, "In Manus," 97.

useful in a rhetorical context, they have become useless in the context of recitation. In other words, youth and ability were a requirement for the efficient use of a literary prosthetic. This explains why when the age of literate workers is mentioned it is always in the context of their youth, as older and "expired" workers would age out because of impairment or disability.

The prosthetic use of literate workers not only illumines their physical vulnerability and how the nature of the profession itself literally expired their bodies. Their corporeal fragility points to their replaceability and their expendable social nature. If they become disabled, they can no longer be productive and if they are no longer productive, they are malfunctioning prosthetics. Given requisite economic means, enslaved literate workers could be substituted infinitely.

Thomas Habinek argued that for ancient Roman authors their "ego was expandible, not limited by the boundaries of a single body. Just as the pronouns 'I' and 'you' could signify 'my slaves and I' or 'you and your slaves', so in practice a slave performed as a prosthesis of his master, even when the master was an esteemed writer."[192] Sarah Blake puts it like this: "…the Roman master is also a different degree of human: he is an amplified person, one that exists noy only in his own physical form, but also in and throughout the slaves and objects that work for, with, and of him."[193]

Enslaved literate workers were not just extensions of the bodies of their masters, enabling physical ability restricted by status or disability, but extensions of their *Self*. As we will see in the next section, the reliance on such workers for the generation of complex theological works such as commentaries and translations went far beyond mere rote dictation and stylistic enhancement.

5 The Works of Us: Prolific Dictation and the Mirage of the Great Commentator

For early Christian workers writing enormous volumes like commentaries, it is well known that they employed literate workers to aid in this work. The most prolific example is, of course, Origen of Alexandria. Descriptions of Origen's use of literate workers appears in Eusebius and the work of Jerome.[194] Eusebius tells us that it was Ambrose of Alexandria who

---

[192] Habinek, "Slavery and Class," 385. Reay calls this the extension of the master's body. Reay, "Agriculture, Writing, and Cato's Aristocratic Self-Fashioning," 349.
[193] Blake, "Now You See Them," 198.
[194] Eusebius, *Hist. eccl.* 6.23.1–2; Jerome, *Vir. ill.* 61.

compelled Origen to write a series of commentaries on all of the Christian scriptures. Ambrose funded this project out of his own finances. Eusebius claims that Origen employs *more* than seven secretaries, who would take turns writing Origen's dictations, in addition to at least seven copyists and other women calligraphers. All in all, this involved a team of at least fifteen people in collaboration with one another.[195]

The passages in Eusebius and Jerome do not explicit note that such individuals were necessary purchased (even if Ambrose is financially responsible for providing them). We know from Paulinus's Life of Ambrose that Ambrose did employ the enslaved workers of others like Probus who had sent his enslaved secretary to work with Ambrose.[196] Jeremiah Coogan suggests that these individuals were enslaved.[197] If they were trained in an in-house *paedagogium* owned by Ambrose, as suggested by Haines-Eitzen, then it is likely that they were enslaved.[198] It is also possible that other literate workers not provided by Ambrose but employed by Origen may have been as well.

As far as their contributions to his overall project, Origen's calligraphers and copyists were not likely to have been involved in the generation and revision of his commentary. Secretaries on the other hand likely contributed more than just efficiency to Origen's work.

We know from Jerome that Ambrose expected work to be daily produced, so much so that Jerome says Origen called Ambrose his "taskmaster."[199] The amount of literate workers that Ambrose has supplied at his own expense proved to be a pressure point, allowing on the one hand Origen to produce a lot of work, but on the other hand intensifying the swiftness by which high-quality commentaries had to be produced by end of day.

Origen does describe the process by which the writing of these commentaries takes place. In an overtly dramatic fashion, Origen speaks about his process of writing amid apparent conflict in Alexandria, possibly to do with new heretical writings that he views are opposed to his understanding of the gospel.[200] Speaking about writing the fifth and sixth books on this commentary of John, Origen mentions his dictation of "the words which

---

[195] When ascertaining the veracity of forged letters written in his name, Athanasius mentions his customary secretary but also his wider team of writers. *Apol. Const.* 11. Jerome also notes the necessity of having multiple literate workers. Preface to *Comm. Ecc.*; *Epist.* 143.
[196] Paulinus of Milan, *Life of Ambrose* 6.21.
[197] Coogan, "Tabular Thinking," 67.
[198] Haines-Eitzen, *Guardians*, 60.
[199] Jerome, *Vir. ill.* 61.
[200] *Comm. Jo.* 6.6–8.

were given us."²⁰¹ A little later, when he is distressed when he becomes aware of these new hostile writings forced upon him by "the enemy" he notes that he had to stop writing because he did not want to write until his mind regained its stability. It just so happens that at that time he "was hindered" because his "accustomed stenographers were not present to take the dictations."²⁰²

Two things are important to note from this passage. The first is that although Origen gives dictation to his literate workers, he seems to view himself (or at least portrays himself in writing to Ambrose) as a kind of passive instrument receiving divine knowledge about the text and then passing it on to his stenographers. As Miriam DeCock argues, "At several points throughout his exegetical homilies, Origen stopped a particular line of interpretation to indicate that the Logos spoke to him in that very moment."²⁰³ The message is given to Origen, and Origen merely transmits it to his literary workers. He, like his literate workers, is merely a vessel.

The second important facet of this passage is that, while he acknowledges that his distress about new heretical writings has stifled his work, the more practical reason for the delay is that his stenographers were not present to write. For one, according to Eusebius and Jerome, we know that he had at least seven stenographers who switched out when they needed to take breaks. We sometimes are made aware of this kind of rotational process in other areas like in a later Carthaginian conference where notaries taking down shorthand would immediately start to transcribe while another set of notaries would continue taking down shorthand.²⁰⁴ Origen later notes how the beginning of book six that he had dictated previously when he was in Alexander not yet been brought to where he currently was.²⁰⁵ As such, Origen begins dictating the rest of the work without consulting what he had previously written. When his work stalls it is because he lacks stenographers or the literate workers who were supposed to manage his books have not brought them to him while he travels. In the absence of books but in the presence of his stenographers, Origen can write. But in the absence of his stenographers, the writing comes to a halt.

But if the content of Origen's commentary merely comes from the divine Logos, why was he not able to write down the material himself in the

---

[201] *Comm. Jo.* 6.8. Translations from Heine, *Commentary on the Gospel*, 170.
[202] *Comm. Jo.* 6.9.
[203] DeCock, "Origen's Sources of Exegetical Authority," 154.
[204] This particular procedure during the Carthaginian conference was an unusual practice notes Graumann because transcription would usually happen after a session had been completed. Graumann, *The Acts of the Early Church Councils*, 171.
[205] *Comm. Jo.* 6.11.

absence of his literary team? Unless we imagine Origen to be incredibly lazy or himself illiterate, the simplest answer is that the divine Logos is *not* the only source for Origen's commentary. Origen's literate workers are not only providing mechanical services to this commentary project, but *intellectual* services as well. The absence of Origen's literary team points not only to his lack of personnel, of which he bemoans to Ambrose, but also to his complete reliance upon them for the writing of his work.[206] Origen does not and *cannot* write without his stenographers present, at least for this commentary project.

One of the growing emphases in scholarship in this area, especially in early Christianity, is the significant role that literate workers played in authoring early Christian works, not just in terms of enabling writing where disability might be a factor or "authoring" as merely a neutral amanuensis who contributes nothing to the work itself but is merely the instrument, the "right arm" of the named author in the past. In the case of Origen as we have analyzed earlier, he is wholly dependent upon his literate workers for the transportation of his books and for the writing of the material itself. In this way, should we really say that these are *Origen's* commentaries? The way that Origen portrays his own literary process is that God gives him the words and the workers merely write it down. But given that Ambrose is funding the writing of these commentaries, the final product could not be, as Jerome put it, merely the first words that came to his head. Quality was expected. The presence of stenographers, writing in shorthand, means that as it was translated from shorthand into long form there would be a process of revision and refinement, likely by both Origen and his literate workers together. From this point of view, it is historically inaccurate to describe the ideas in these commentaries as being authored by Origen alone. They are a likely a product made through an essential collaboration between him and his literary team.[207]

When we erase the participation of Origen's literary workers, we perpetuate a myth about Origen as a Great Author, the sole genius individual who has shaped the development of Christianity. What Origen's use of literate workers tells us, however, is something different. Origen's work – the archiving, the writing, the revision, the reproduction, and publication – depended upon literate workers, some who arguably occupied positions of

---

[206] Origen argues that he does not have enough resources to finish the project: "After counting up what is at our disposal, we see that we do not possess what is needed to complete the structure." *Comm. Jo.* 6.6.

[207] Even Jerome mentions how his work depends on having a sufficient number of secretarial workers. *Ep.* 143.

coauthorship (or perhaps what in today's terminology would be considered ghostwriting).[208]

At the same time, from a theological angle, Origen is also heavily dependent upon divine inspiration for his content. In this way, being both reliant upon the divine and the human, Origen's commentaries are not his works alone but the work of a larger literate community. This should give us pause about the way we think about the work of other prolific authors, such as Augustine, Jerome, or John Chrysostom. In early Christianity, the ability to write and publish vast amounts of work cannot have been done without collaboration with literate workers. As Harald Hagendahl argued over fifty years ago: "such productivity was impossible without labour-saving means."[209] This is even acknowledged among non-Christian Roman authors like Pliny. Sarah Blake asks, "Without these slaves to hand, would Pliny have been able to produce such a prodigious amount of prose? Decidedly not. 'Pliny the Productive Author' is not simply a man, but more a machine that includes many different parts: Pliny himself, multiple personal slaves, and their inanimate writing materials."[210] In other words, the longevity and historical influence of early Christian authors such as Origen, Augustine, Jerome, or Chrysostom would not have happened had they not had access to early Christian literate workers. These authors exist in a wider matrix of teams consisting of enslaved or formerly enslaved workers that were not only instruments but also agents.

The collaborative literary relationship did not apply only to those who were writing large bodies of work (like commentaries) but also for those composing simple literary products. The Roman poet Ausonius, a Christian in the fourth century CE, waxes poetic about the prescient abilities of his stenographer to the point where the author argues that his literate worker knows intimately the author's own mind.[211] The passage is significant enough to quote in full as it expresses how even ancient "authors" viewed their literate workers as synonymous with themselves:

> Hi, boy! My secretary, skilled in dashing shorthand, make haste and come! Open your folding tablets wherein a world of words is compassed in a few signs and finished off as it were a single phrase. I ponder works of generous scope; and thick and fast like hail the words tumble off

---

[208] So Moss, *God's Ghostwriters*.
[209] "Eine solche Produktion wäre ohne arbeitssparende Mittel unmöglich gewsen." Hagendahl, "Die Bedeutung der Stenographie," 29.
[210] Blake, "Now You See Them," 194.
[211] On whether Ausonius was a Christian, see Chin, *Grammar*, 49 and the scholarship cited on 199 n. 63.

my tongue. And yet your ears are not at fault nor your page crowded, and your right hand, moving easily, speeds over the waxen surface of your tablet. When I declaim, as now, at greatest speed, talking in circles round my theme, you have the thoughts of my heart already set fast in wax almost before they are uttered. I would my mind had given me power to think as swiftly as you outstrip me when I speak, and as your dashing hand leaves my words behind.

Who, prithee, who is he who has betrayed me? Who has already told you what I was but now thinking to say? What thefts are these that your speeding hand perpetrates in the recesses of my mind? How come things in so strange an order that what my tongue has not yet vented comes to your ears? No teaching ever gave you this gift, nor was ever any hand so quick at swift stenography: Nature endowed you so, and God gave you this gift to know beforehand what I would speak, and to intend the same that I intend. (Evelyn-White, LCL 96, 25–27).

Ausonius highlights the sheer prowess of his stenographer, commenting on his skill, ability, speed, and accuracy. For Ausonius, his literate worker's ability to work at such great speeds outpaces his own ability to speak the words. Put another way, his stenographer's ability is premonitory, working and intuiting faster than the words of his master.[212] It borders on the divinatory, the oracular, the prophetic. This is so much the case that Ausonius notes how his stenographer is able to penetrate his mind and these thoughts before he even can think them, thieving his ideas and causing his mind to betray him. Ausonius attributes this ability not to education but to nature and to God who has given it as a gift to know before even Ausonius is able to speak what it is that he wants to say. What is important in this dynamic is that the stenographer shares not only thought, idea, and word but also *intention*.

Ausonius's sentiment here is romanticized. It is not that his stenographer actually as telepathic abilities to write down Ausonius's thoughts before he utters a word. At the same time, however, the elision between author and literate worker and the ability of the stenographer to access the author's thoughts and intentions blurs the line between authorship. As Ella Grunberger-Kirsh argues, "Stenographical training turned a student into an author's second self, even as it made enslaved stenographers ever more unknowable to their masters."[213] I would argue further: it is not merely that the literate worker is an extension of the

---

[212] Not dissimilar to a similar expression by Martial, *Ep.* 14.208: "Though the words speed, the hand is faster than they. The right hand has finished its work, while the tongue has more to do" (Bailey, LCL 380, page 219).

[213] Grunberger-Kirsh, "Etched into the Soul," 63.

author (as argued in the last section) but also conceived of being a part of the very same mind of the author themselves, an extension of the authorial Self, sometimes accessing the thoughts in a quicker fashion than the dictator themselves.

This further problematizes the misconception that literate workers were merely vessels through which authorial ideas passed through and were inscribed. Rather, Ausonius's comments suggest that the literate workers could be understood as participating in the authorial act itself at the level of mind and intention. This does not mean that all ancient writers thought the same about the abilities and roles of literate workers. We might recall Cornelius Nepos's opinion about Romans viewing scribes as mere hirelings (and thus vessels) as opposed to Greeks whose secretaries come from elite families and are thus knowledgeable (and more participatory) in secretarial work.[214] Still, however, even though not all literate workers *were* viewed with the same level of estimate as Ausonius's stenographer, it nevertheless allows *us* to understand the rightful authorial role of literate workers in the generation of early Christian literature. We can acknowledge the truncated perspective of enslaved authorship in the past while recognizing the historical and practical reality of enslaved authorship at the same time.

What we have seen in this section so far is that ancient named authors relied heavily upon their literate workers to contribute, improve, and shape the documents that they were writing. But what about those authors who claim *they* are more principally involved? Some like Jerome, for example, portray themselves as more heavy handed. In his description of his use of secretarial workers it is often the case that his work is sent out before it is refined in style, so much so that some of his readers complain.

As noted previously, it is the case that sometimes, given time, literate workers improved the style of notes that are written. In Jerome's case, the way he characterizes his own shaping of the style of his writing, and often, his lack of shaping, suggests that, in his use of literary workers, he was the one who was primarily making decisions about improvements and the shaping of the work.[215] How can we know that this is true, that authors like Jerome are wholly involved and not substantially relying on their workers for the production of this literature?

One way to verify this is to think about the amount of work such authors were able to produce with their teams. In other words, we need

---

[214] *Eum.* 18.4–5.
[215] For the largest overview of Jerome's production of literature from material to publication, see Arns, *La technique du livre* esp. 37–76 related to dictation and stenography.

to think not just about the practically of writing and revision but also the speed at which the production of work can be finished. Augustine once talked about his literary productivity during travel from September 11 to December 1st, dictating 6,000 lines.[216] During this period he wrote at least four letters, one book, and six sermons (for the latter he reserved Saturday and Sunday evenings).

We find a similar example of immense textual production in Jerome's work as well. In a preface to two bishops, Cromatius and Heliodorus, concerning his translation of the books of Solomon, Jerome notes how it took three days in the summer of 398 for him, his secretaries and copyists, to finish translating all of Proverbs, Ecclesiastes, and the Song of Songs. Conceptions of Jerome's dictational method have, in the past, relegated the lion's share of the intellectual work onto the father himself. Schlumberger argued nearly fifty years ago that Jerome would spend as much time as possible before hand absorbing literature before dictating quickly.[217]

According to the Cheltenham canon, the rough number of *stichoi* (lines) of the books of Solomon (including Wisdom and Ben Sira as they were associated with Solomon in early Christianity) is 6500.[218] Even if we hypothesize that Proverbs, Ecclesiastes, and the Song of Songs only makes up perhaps 30–40 percent of that *stichoi* total we are still dealing with about 80–120 columns of text (based on roughly 20–25 lines per column, cf. Codex Amiatinus) that not only need to be written but *translated* from Hebrew into Latin in three days. In comparison to Augustine, what would have taken Augustine and his team forty days to complete, Jerome claims to have completed including *translation* in three days.[219]

The question of Jerome's ability to work in Hebrew and the extent to which he knew it has been a contested over the years. The study of Michael Graves argues that while our ancient sources place Jerome in contact with Jewish teachers (who taught him the alphabet and vocalization) and other experts in the community whom he consulted for particularly difficult texts (e.g., Chronicles, Job), Jerome's end products (his commentaries and translation of the Vulgate) consistently over almost a two-decade

---

[216] Augustine, *Ep.* 23α.3 (Divjak letters). Translation available from Halton and Eno, *Saint Augustine*.
[217] Schlumberger, "Non scribo sed dicto," 224.
[218] According to Hugh Houghton: "the standard unit for measuring the length of Latin texts was one line of hexameter verse, as found in Vergil." Houghton, "The Fourth Century," 21.
[219] Jerome and Augustine may have had a different number of literary workers. This, however, magnifies the problem as we will see below since if he had more and could complete translation faster it would require a larger set of very skilled interpreters who could work in multiple languages.

period show that he had facility with the language even if he did not have the same kind of fluency as other Jewish experts in late antiquity.[220] It is well established that Jerome also heavily consulted Greek versions of the Hebrew Bible (e.g., Aquila, Symmachus, and Theodotion) when translating and commenting on books from the HB.[221] Graves also shows that Jerome does make judgments about the HB text independent from Greek sources (even if he always consults Greek *recentiores*). The question is whether these judgments come from him or consultation with literate workers who may have been familiar with Hebrew (to the same or greater extent than him).

Graves' thorough analysis is very helpful but one facet of Jerome's ability with Hebrew that he overlooks is the heavy reliance Jerome had on literate workers. Jerome might have had *knowledge* of Hebrew but what about the practicalities of reading and translating Hebrew? We know that some early Christian literate workers were skilled in translating various languages (e.g., conciliary secretaries) and so ability to work in Hebrew would likely have been within their skill-set.[222] Additionally, we know that at least since 387, Jerome – by this time possible 40–45 years old – has been open about both his inability to write and also his fading eyesight.[223] As Jerome's eyesight impairment worsened it is very likely he approached a level of illiteracy where he would have had to rely increasingly on his literate workers who may have had a "greater liberty to edit" his words.[224] While Cain is probably right that Jerome "strategically voiced such complains in order to heroicize himself as an embattled scholar who has worn out his eyes and body prematurely through excessive study and asceticism," this was him likely capitalizing on a real deteriorating physical condition.[225] Indeed, Hagendahl calculated that at least sixty of Jerome's works in the late period of his life were done via dictation.[226]

For Jerome to be translating works from Hebrew into Latin 11 years later, with his eyesight worsening over time, even if he supplied the interpretations himself, he would likely still have been reliant on

---

[220] Graves, *Jerome's Hebrew Philology*, 76–127.
[221] For example, his preface to his *Comm. Ecc.* and *Epist.* 32.1.
[222] See also the next section's discussion on Bishop Selinus, formerly a secretary, who had the ability to teach in both Greek and Gothic.
[223] Mentioned in the preface to book 3 to his *Comm. Gal.*
[224] On the latter point, Moss, "The Secretary," 44.
[225] Cain, *Jerome's Commentaries*, 11–12. On passages where Jerome mentions his illness, see Arns, *La technique du livre*, 42–43.
[226] Hagendahl, "Die Bedeutung der Stenographie," 30.

literate workers who could read the Hebrew text to him. If they had to read the Hebrew, then they would have had to have been able to work in this language as well to an equal if not more proficient degree than Jerome.[227] If his literate workers had the ability to read Hebrew, then it is also plausible that while in consultation with the Greek versions or members of the community, Jerome also relied upon his literate workers to help revise or provide meaning and help in translating large bodies of Hebrew text into Latin. The fact that this task was able to be done in *three days* with Jerome – given his own physical disabilities, his limited albeit sufficient knowledge of Hebrew, and the presence of literate workers – demonstrates that his literate workers were not merely supplemental to Jerome's translation work but that they were essential for its completion. Jerome's multi-volume works were not products that relied only on him, even if his name is the only one attached to the work. They were most certainly a work of "us."

The need to rely on Jerome's physical disability to prove that he would have had to rely on his literate workers later on in his life already betrays a problematic default in scholarship, that is the burden of proof is on those who think literate workers could have contributed *anything* to the creation of early Christian texts. In other words, *unless proven otherwise*, these workers were merely vessels transmitting symbols and converting sound into written form. But as Martin Goodman argues regarding Jewish scribal activity: "Perhaps the two roles of scribes, as writers and interpreters, were mutually reinforcing. An expert *sofer* who was trusted to produce valid manuscripts for worship might well also be a learned exegete of the biblical texts he assiduously copied."[228] If this might be the case for Jewish literate workers, why not also potentially for Christian ones as well? Especially among those who later became bishops or ecclesial leaders. The writing, editing, correction, and formulation of material for theologically prodigious writers like Origen or Augustine or Jerome would have been a formative experience. Those who were able to work over multiple years must certainly have been able to learn and become experts in the translations, commentaries, and texts on which they worked. As the

---

[227] In his *Prol. Tobit*, Jerome mentions how he had someone familiar with both Aramaic and Hebrew explain the text to him in Hebrew and, with the help of a notary, he explained the Hebrew explanations in Latin. It may simply have been the case that the notary was merely scribing precisely what Jerome had written down, but it is also possible that his worker, familiar with Hebrew, might have also suggested notes and revisions based on what they heard the bilingual aid say.

[228] Goodman, "Texts, Scribes and Power in Roman Judea," 89.

next section shows, accumulative secretarial work carried forward and the bishops who were once formerly secretaries are examples of some of the theological expertise of early Christian literate workers. Unless we presume that these workers had an intellectual capacity that reset itself with every new project, we must presume that such workers carried what they learned and what they wrote with them to every continuing project. In this way, it is appropriate to shift the burden of proof on to those who think literate workers did not contribute anything to their literary productions. It is they who need to prove the static intellectual nature and ability of an expert class of literary workers whose day-in-day-out was the production of intense theological work.

As Candida Moss argues, "authorship is not a solitary activity and is, thus, always collaborative."[229] Or to contradict an often-asserted mantra of some scholarship, that literate workers did not perform authorial work in antiquity, with in Jerome's translations we see that his authorial work would not have been possible without his secretaries.[230] The expertise of Jerome's literate workers would not necessarily be unusual in the ancient world. Indeed, as Harriet Flower has argued, in the ancient Roman world we have examples of enslaved persons who were very skilled, like Daphnis, the highest paid enslaved worker in Roman history, who authored multiple historiographical works.[231] It was the case then, as Haines-Eitzen observed nearly two decades ago, that the ability that early Christian literate workers had to manipulate and change early Christian literature shows "a certain power over the texts they copied."[232] Literate workers, enslaved or otherwise, enabled early Christian theological production.

6 Pathway to the Episcopate: Secretarial Work as a Precursor to an Office

Secretaries, free(d) and enslaved, were not necessarily locked into this profession for the entirety of their life. If they did not move on because of impairment or disability, it could be but one position in a career that began among the lower administrative ranks and rose to higher political and ecclesial ranks, even to the role of bishops in late antique Christianity. This was not just the case in the late centuries BCE but also through

---

[229] Moss, "The Secretary," 22.
[230] Compare Ehrman, *Forgery and Counter-Forgery* and the critique by Moss, "The Secretary," 29.
[231] Flower, *The Most Expensive Slave*, 101.
[232] Haines-Eitzen, *Guardians*, 16.

the third and fourth centuries CE.²³³ Secretaries could rise to other positions like prefect, *magister officiorum* (chief-marshal of the court), and even consul.²³⁴

In this section we will briefly examine the career trajectories of three early Christian bishops who began in some capacity as secretaries and worked their way up into higher positions. Nowhere is it mentioned from any of these figures whether they were enslaved at one point, but it is likely that they were and were eventually freedmen as they grew in age and in position. For example, in one of Gregory I's letters, a certain enslaved person, Thomas, is manumitted in order to serve as a notary for the church.²³⁵ Teilter once argued that because of the cost of purchasing an enslaved literate worker was high, "as the fourth century progressed bishops probably tended more and more to select their *notarii* from the clergy."²³⁶ At the same time, however, we have evidence of multiple clergy being secretaries before they were ecclesial leaders. Indeed, the ability to be promoted may have attracted enslaved workers in the first place, although we should be careful of assuming that their rise up ecclesiastical ranks freed them from the lifelong tendrils of enslavement even after manumission.

The church historian Sozomen records a dispute among Arian Christians about whether God the Father could be called Father before the existence of the Son. One of the parties, led by a certain Marinus, was supported by Selinus who was a bishop from among the Goths.²³⁷ Sozomen calls these peoples "barbarians." Selinus who at the time of this ongoing controversy was a bishop had succeeded his mentor, Wulfila (Ulfilas/Urphilas) a fourth-century Gothic bishop who is famous among ancient Christian historians for overseeing the translation of the Christian scriptures into the Gothic language (although his actual involvement is questioned by historians).²³⁸ Sozomen notes that Selinus was once the secretary of Ulfilas and, like his mentor, also taught in both Greek and Gothic in their churches. If Wulfila was indeed involved in the translation of the scriptures into Gothic, then Selinus would likely have been one of the literate workers who was also involved in this task, since he was able to read both Greek (the language of the New Testament) and Gothic. For the purposes

---

[233] For example, Plutarch, *Comp. Eum. Sert.* 1.3.
[234] Amm. Marc. 17.14.2, 26.5.14, 26.7.2. 28.2.5.
[235] *Ep.* 6.12.
[236] Teitler, *Notarii and exceptores*, 91. Harriet Flower has recently written on the highly literate enslaved worker Daphnis who sold for 700,000 sestertii. Flower, "The Most Expensive Slave in Rome."
[237] *Hist. eccl.* 7.17.
[238] See, for example, Ratkus, "Greek ἀρχιερεύς in Gothic translation."

of this section, however, it is simply important to note that Selinus began as a literate worker with the bishop and eventually replaced Wulfila him as bishop. This tells us about the future trajectories and opportunities available to literate workers; there was a level of limited social mobility that was available to them. At the same time, it was not simply the literary skill that made such workers qualified for these senior positions later on but the range of their abilities. Selinus not only shared Wulfila's literary prowess but, according to Sozomen, he was able to preach in Gothic Christian communities in Greek and in the Gothic languages. Sozomen also notes that Selinus's opinion was held in esteem by Arian Gothics.

Although not every literate worker would have had the exact same career journey, the path from secretary to bishop would not have been a straight line. Elsewhere Sozomen details the career of Proclus of Constantinople (fifth century CE).[239] An avid reader and a student of rhetoric when he was young, Proclus became Atticus the bishop's secretary. After he had progressed, he was promoted to deacon, then to presbyter, and then later ordained by Sisinnius to be bishop of Cyzicus. He later took on the episcopal chair of Constantinople. His proximity to Atticus allowed him to imitate all of the bishop's virtue, even exceeding his mentor's own patience and gentleness and kindness. While in the case of Selinus, we saw the literate worker's proximity allowed him to share and participate in their master's literary prowess, with Proclus we see that proximity was a matter of conveying and communicating perceived Christian character and behavior. For Proclus, these characteristics that learned from working closely with Atticus became useful in his later episcopal positions when he dealt with people, with controversies, and with other religious mediation.

One of the more vivid biographical portrayals about a literate worker who became a bishop in early Christian sources that we have concerns the condemned ultra-Arian heretic Eunomius who flourished around the end of the fourth century CE. Gregory of Nyssa says that Eunomius' father was a farmer and that Eunomius, not wanting to be uneducated like his father, taught himself how to write in shorthand.[240] Before long he was employed in family members housing, trading boarding for his abilities as a writer, tutoring others and wanting to be an orator. Later Eunomius finds himself in close association with Aetius, bishop of Antioch. Theodoret says that Eunomius used to call Aetius his "master" but it is not clear if he was ever owned by Aetius or if this was merely

---

[239] *Hist. eccl.* 7.41.
[240] *C. Eun.* 1.6.

an honorific.²⁴¹ Sozomen says that Aetius was Eunomius's teacher.²⁴² Philostorgius, a great admirer of Eunomius, argues that both Aetius and Eunomius taught and learned from one another.²⁴³ It is only Socrates of Constantinople who notes that Eunomius had actually been Aetius's amanuensis.²⁴⁴

The proximity of Enomius to Aetius is clearly a point of tension for writers arguing against the views of both figures. As we saw with both Selinus and Proclus, proximity to Christian leaders shaped the character, teaching, and ability of literate workers – sometimes for good and, in the case of Eunomius, sometimes for perceived bad (heresy). Proximity to heresiarchs brought about suspicion and the indictment of close associates, usually that they likely held the same views as their teachers but may be hiding them from plain view. In any case the career of Eunomius progresses from shorthand writer to secretary, eventually to deacon and then eventually to bishop of Cyzicus after Eleusius.²⁴⁵

The skills that some literate workers learned serving ecclesial masters often gave them the tools and skills to succeed at higher levels of church leadership. At the same time, that we have career trajectories at all tells us a bit about enslaved literate workers in Christian communities and the kinds of potential aspirations that they had for their own lives. They did not only become persons once they had received a bishopric but were persons with developing hopes and dreams even while serving in the unmentioned ranks of ecclesial orders.

7 Invisibility, Critical Fabulation, and Recovering Literate Workers in Early Christian History

Origen. Augustine. Jerome.

Early Christian authors cast long shadows. So stygian are these shadows that they obscure the many, often enslaved, literate workers who not only helped them produce the text from a technological perspective but also from an ideational, content, and linguistic perspective. One of the significant historiographic problems in all of history, but especially in ancient history is the recovery of the perspectives of those who were enslaved. Ancient historians often characterize these workers as "invisible." Present

---

²⁴¹ Theodoret, *Hist. eccl.* 2.19, 25.
²⁴² Sozomen, *Hist. eccl.* 6.27.
²⁴³ In Photius's epitome of Philostorgius, *Hist. eccl.* 3.20. For translation in English, see Amidon, *Philostorgius*.
²⁴⁴ Socrates, *Hist. eccl.* 2.35
²⁴⁵ Theodoret, *Hist. eccl.* 2.25.

in iconographic motifs or when a master asks for a quick dictation, but only from an enslavers' perspective, rarely from their own, if at all. This pattern in ancient classics carries over into the study of early Christian literate workers. As Candida Moss recently argues, "The primary reason that secretaries are absent from our accounts of ancient authorial work is that ancient discourse about enslaved labour renders those responsible for it largely invisible."[246] Joseph Howley argues that the subjectivity of ancient literate workers is "beyond recovery."[247] Coogan, Moss, and Howley argue that the occlusion of literate workers from view has to do with the despotic "enslaver discourses" that "maintained that enslaved people were tools or body parts through which the enslaver enacted his will."[248] The rhetoric here is meant to problematize, rightfully so, the idea that ancient authors were sole literary genius is an illusion perpetuated by the enslaver perspective of the sources themselves. It is designed to help bring to light the presence and contributions of workers who helped make the greater authors of the past great.

In order to recover enslaved literate perspectives some scholars, like Candida Moss, have turned to critical fabulation as a partial solution, an epistemological framework used in concert with other historical and materialist methodologies.[249] Moss writes, "This process involves reading into the gaps, engaging in what historian of Atlantic slavery Saidiya Hartman calls critical fabulation: a form of history-telling that is imaginative, and not untrue. The evidence is fragmented but is itself evidence."[250] The concern here is not the use of imagination in reconstructing history; anyone familiar with historiography over the past hundred years and any metacriticism of the field knows that every historian's imagination is involved whether they are aware of it or not. Neither is the concern with the kind of narrative imagination that can be used to read plausible history into the gaps, which is the mode that Moss uses throughout her work. My question is about why fabulation is necessary.

On the one hand, the focus of scholars like Moss is on an earlier archive than the remit of this volume. New Testament and early Christian literature up to the second and early third centuries offers far sparser

---

[246] Moss, "The Secretary," 36.
[247] Howley, "In Ancient Rome," 23.
[248] Coogan, Moss, and Howley, "Introduction," 2–3.
[249] Moss, *God's Ghostwriters*, 3–7; Moss, "The Secretary"; Moss, "Fashioning Mark."
[250] Moss, *God's Ghostwriters*, 3. Coogan, Moss, and Howley also draw upon others such as Michel-Rolph Trouillot and Marisa Fuentes. Coogan, Moss, and Howley, "Introduction."

accounts of literate workers in comparison to the more plentiful sources available among early Christian documents from the third through sixth centuries CE. Given the difference in the nature of available evidence, it is certainly the case that different evidence requires different historiographic methods suited to the specifics of each archive.

On the other hand, Moss's use of critical fabulation does not substantially affect the conclusions of her work which are based on detailed albeit theoretically informed analysis of historical data and comparative evidence. My critique of the use of critical fabulation here is not intended to denigrate what are absolutely essential historical tools. Neither is what I present in this section or this Element diametrically opposed to that task. Rather, these critiques are constructive, done with the intent to inspire readers to take up and find solutions to a few methodological shortcomings that currently limit the study of literate workers in early Christian literature. Moss's work is historically sound and compelling. What is of concern is the way that critical fabulation as a framework in this particular area of ancient enslaved literate work might actually *limit* the extent of her conclusions. In other words, Moss's historical conclusions should be taken further but are being held back with the use of critical fabulation as an answer to the so-called invisibility of literate workers in the ancient world.

The key question is one posed by Moss herself: "After the perspectives and experiences of enslaved workers there to be found, or have they been thoroughly overwritten by those who hold power?"[251] This is a question is raised not only by ancient historians but historians of Atlantic enslavement. The perilous task of the historian is to find the right balance given the archive of material that we have. On the one hand, as Niall McKeown argues, "we must be careful not to 'rescue' the voice of the ancient slave by making it a distorted version of our own"[252] On the other hand, should be presume that the ancient evidence written about and *by* enslaved literate workers was predominantly "overwritten by those who hold power"?

Critical fabulation was formulated by Saidiya Hartman particularly because of the nature of the enslavement archive with which she was working.[253] Hartman was frustrated by the one-sided and viscerally violent portrays of enslaved women during the time, especially in crossing the Atlantic, and in seeking to rescue the impossible, the counter-histories that the extant archive could not describe their experiences, she developed critical

---

[251] Moss, *God's Ghostwriters*, 3.
[252] McKeown, *The Invention of Ancient Slavery?* 163.
[253] The key theoretical overview of Hartman's conceptualization of critical fabulation can be found in Hartman, "Venus in Two Acts."

fabulation as a narratival way of providing a non-enslaved biographical perspective of these women's experiences.[254] But some critics of the approach, like Vincent Brown, have cautioned that it can sometimes overlook or ignore the voices of the enslaved that we do have in the archive.[255] The use of critical fabulation has also tended toward a complete mistrust of archives concerning enslavement. Trevor Burnard notes that these uses tend "toward a nihilism about an archive seen in Foucauldian terms as immensely powerful when it can always be read in ways that go against the archival grain."[256] In other words, the way users deploy critical fabulation involves jettisoning the archive as a whole. This may be legitimate in certain areas of enslavement studies, especially in studying trans-Atlantic enslavement. It is unclear if this is applicable to the study of enslavement in the ancient Mediterranean world.

Recent work by classics scholarship on ancient enslavement have been pressing against this invisibility metanarrative in historical scholarship as well. The work of Sandra Joshel and Lauren Petersen is illustrative:

> Indeed, the slaves of ancient Roma have little narrative of their own. Rather, they are participants in their masters' narratives, absorbed into and necessary for them. Yet through epitaphs and the veil of slaveholders' literature and law, scholars have made the conditions of slaves' lives, family relations, and work visible. This body of work has been vital to our project. However, the words of slaveholders, descriptions of what slaves did or should do and did not or should not do in houses, streets, work spaces, and villas, often feel disconnected from the archaeological settings that we can associate with those descriptions. Our project has been to put slaves in motion in the spaces and places where they lived and worked. Where scholarly practices unwittingly un-see slaves in the material record, we have tried to weave text and archaeology into a project of seeing.[257]

Joshel and Petersen are not alone as others like Sarah Richlin have sought to recover "the thoughts and feelings of slaves" in ancient Roman drama.[258] Recently my colleague Katherine Huemoeller argues from a middle ground, acknowledging that "first-hand" sources concerning enslavement in the ancient world should also not be merely taken at face

---

[254] For a recent overview of the contribution of Hartman and others in the wider context of global enslavement, see Burnard, *Writing the History of Global Slavery*, 51–56.
[255] Brown, "Social Death," 1239–40.
[256] Burnard, *Writing the History of Global Slavery*, 54.
[257] Joshel and Petersen, *The Material Life of Roman Slaves*, 220.
[258] Richlin, *Slave Theater in the Roman Republic*, 67.

value but should not be excluded *in toto*.[259] As scholars of enslavement, Sophie White and Trevor Burnard argue "that we should not dismiss fragmented testimony as 'a mere body of data', enslaved people were involved in the production of their testimonies; and we cannot just discard slave testimonies because they 'fail to fit the overly high standard of literary authenticity required by those who want to hear an unadulterated voice emanating from a slave's consciousness'."[260] The same caution toward overlooking enslaved perspectives in our historical archive for literate workers in early Christianity should be exercised.

A number of previous sections in this Element have sought to show their visibility in our sources and raise further questions for research. In Section 1 we encountered the physical appearance of ancient literate workers, details about their embodiment, thee places they slept, the social organization of their working communities. If enslaved workers differed in ethnicity or religion from their Christian masters, how did that affect the works that were created? To what extent could such literate workers keep ties to the cultures of their homeland, if they had any memory of it at all? We encountered the disabling nature of literate work. How long could literate workers work until their bodies expired on them? What means of healthcare and medicine were available to alleviate chronic pain and physical impairment? We encountered both men and women working as literate workers in the ancient world, even in early Christianity. How was their experience different and to what extent would literate workers be harmed sexually by their Christian owners? We encountered the diverse ages of children trained as secretaries and stenographers. Would they have viewed their masters as paternalistic figures? Would they feel kinship toward them? Would they fear them?

In Section 2 we thought about the need for ancient historians to take into consideration Jewish evidence of literate workers. By truncating our Mediterranean archive, what enslaved perspectives and experiences might we be missing from the works of Philo and Josephus, both of whom certainly deployed literary workers, or members of the Bar Kokhba revolt? Might we be able to draw analogies between the way early Christians used literate workers in ancient Palestine in late antiquity with literary production in ancient tannaitic and amoraic literature?

In Section 3 we thought about the role literate workers played in church councils and important judicial gatherings. We encountered their

---

[259] Huemoeller, "Lost and (Not) Found."
[260] Burnard, *Writing the History of Global Slavery*, 44.

spatial experiences of the space, the noise rising from all different parties, the feverish switching out from stenography to transcription while their peers moved into place to continue taking dictation. We also encountered some key moments where ecclesial decisions about heresy, dogma, and doctrine depended upon the work of literary workers. Even while many are nameless, they were an integral part of the development of early Christian theological formulations. Even if they were enslaved, they nevertheless exercised a tremendous unrecognized amount of agency over the creation of what becomes theological pillars for Christian communities worldwide.

In Section 4 we analyzed the prosthetic nature of the relationship between literate workers and their masters. They were extensions of the self of their owners or leaders, sometimes serving to offset physical disability and other times as instruments of convenience. If enslaved, although they lacked agency, they still exerted an influence as extensions of their master's body, even if such influence was the byproduct of coercion. In fact, they exerted an agency that may have been impossible (or inconvenient) for their masters, exceeding them in physical ability. The proximity of literate worker to master perhaps challenges simplistic notions of agency that we as historians bring to the texts in the past.

In Section 5 we examined the essential work of literate workers with early Christian writers whose prodigious bodies of writing required their expertise. We find sometimes that they work is teams of multiples (in the case of Origen). Over twenty years ago Kim Haines-Eitzen drew our attention to scribal networks across communities. What about scribal networks within a household? What kind of community did Origen's literate workers have with one another? Were they family? Did they have social ties? How might they have supported each other? In this section we also looked at times when ancient authors recognized the surpassing technical skills of literate workers, surpassing even the dictation of the orator himself. How might Ausonius's secretary have felt about his master's praise of his literate skill? Did he think his master thought of him equally? Did he blush? Did he grow afraid, perhaps adjusting his ability so that the velocity of his stenography matched the tempo of his master's dictation? It is also in this section where we encounter Jerome's growing need, given his visual impairment, for literate workers to translate and comment exegetically on ancient texts. Did Jerome's literate workers actually become frustrated with his sometimes brutally slow and simplistic dictations? Did they ever become frustrated that he took credit for their hard translation work? Or were they encultured to be silent, the idea of possession or having their named attached to a work beaten out of their conscious mind?

In Section 6 we encountered the ecclesial trajectories that some secretaries had in early Christianity. They could become deacons, elders, and bishops. In an early Christian context, there could be something that enslaved workers might hope for beyond manumission, service and status and (relative) stability and influence in early Christian communities. Even if mediated through an enslaver perspective, there are nevertheless glimmers of social mobility, the potential experiences of enslaved persons rising in the ranks of early Christianity. Is that so hard to imagine? In this Element I have raised snapshots that generate further questions where the experiences and subjectivity of enslaved or formerly enslaved literate workers *may* be found, if one is willing to look.

In light of these Sections, there are a few constructive methodological proposals that I have that concern approaching literate workers, especially enslaved persons, in early Christian history and literature. The first is that there is a presumption among scholarship that the named author's voices are dominant and retained in the extant texts; it is published (usually) in their name, and they had editorial control over what was said. We would not however say the same thing about editors and authors today. It is a known fact that editors (depending on the genre of writing) can edit and change aspects of texts written by authors and do, to a varying degree, have final say in whether a manuscript is ready to be published or not. This of course depends on the type of publication but in my own experience from journal publications to monographs, this work can and does happen.[261] In light of this practice, we would not say, however, that we lack access to the author's ideas and voice. In fact, in modern publishing, it is the editor's voice who goes unacknowledged, though we who are involved in the process know it remains in some form. There are sentences, phrases and sometimes whole sections that have been penned by the editor that were not originally written by the named author. This analogy is useful for thinking about the recoverability of enslaved/formerly enslaved literate workers from the extant texts. The baseline is that the perspectives and ideas of these literate workers cannot be recovered from our texts with confidence. As I argued at the end of Section 5, the burden of proof rests on those who wish to prove it otherwise.

Despite all the arguments about these workers as authors and thinkers themselves and their influence on texts, scholars still emphasize their invisibility. Drawing upon Saidiya Hartman, Jeremiah Coogan argues that it is

---

[261] I have had phrases changed, whole sections improved, and words inserted that I myself did not write – all of which have improved pieces, and I am grateful!

"'an act of chance or disaster,' that makes the enslaved figure visible."[262] I think that it is not only chance or disaster that makes enslaved figures visible, but epistemological shifts. I suggest that such literate workers are not invisible nor imperceivable from our ancient sources. Rather, it is our preconceptions about literary production – preconceptions that have been shaped by the ancient enslaver's perspective – that veils our perception into the past. In other words, it is not merely a case of "visible" extant evidence, the marks of literate workers, their first-person perspectives, or their names explicitly attached to a document that would make such workers visible. I am not advocating for a historical method that isolates and separates the distinct voices of literate worker and named author from one another. This task is impossible and, I think, unnecessary. What is needed is not a sieve, an instrument like the criteria of authenticity used in the study of the historical Jesus. What is needed is a different epistemological orientation.

Chance Bonar observes of scholarship in the ancient Mediterranean that, "Orthonymous texts and their authorial claims are often treated as an unexamined default."[263] Up to the present day, the rule among scholarship has been to ascribe the origin of the content of ancient works to the named author unless proven others. I suggest that it should be the other way around. We should ascribe the origin of the content of ancient worlds to named authors *and* their literate workers unless proven otherwise.[264] With this perspectival change, we see that the workers are visible all the time, if we have the eyes to see them, just as Joshel and Petersen argue above.[265] The very documents we have access to in the past, their copies, and the

---

[262] Coogan, "Notes," 164. I am far less pessimistic about the recoverability of ancient literate workers: "I hesitate to think that modern scholars can construct a history that adequately grapples with the absences. There is often little we can say about the lives, work, and agency of enslaved people in the Roman Mediterranean. Long histories of violence, both in antiquity and in the intervening centuries, have often made their creativity, their labor, and their agency imperceptible to use." Coogan, "Notes," 165.

[263] Bonar, *The Author*, 1.

[264] A wonderful example of this can be found in the work of Bonar on Paul the apostle's letters, *The Author*, 25–29.

[265] Recently Joseph Howley has recently remarked somewhat optimistically, "It is common to lament the lack of traces of enslaved experience in elite literature, but, as I will argue, a reading that centers book slavery reveals more of those traces than we might see otherwise." Howley, "Despotics," 25. Javal Coleman and Dan-el Padilla Peralta also acknowledge a limited level of recoverability of lived experiences from our sources: "Nevertheless, by carefully sifting through different iterations of this rhetoric and their convergence on the language of utility and trust, we can better explicate some of the structural conditions that shaped the lived experience of enslaved and formerly enslaved individuals – even if pinpointing the specifics of those lived experiences proves challenging." Coleman and Padilla Peralta, "Rhetorics," 251.

few autographs still preserved, are *their* products, often written with *their* hands. In seeking to reinstate literate workers in our understanding of literary production the cultural vestiges of the Great Author paradigm still pressure us to forget workers who are there. Literate workers are not invisible. It is only *our own* presuppositions that obscure them. When we deconstruct our epistemological conceptions of literary production and authorship it is easy to see them hunched over next to named authors, writing in tandem. There is a difference between invisibility and awareness; the subjectivities of the workers are there; we have just not always been paying attention to reality of their presence.[266]

With enslavement being so widespread in the ancient world and with the manumission of many enslaved persons, it is also tempting to think about enslavement as transient and temporary. But as much scholarship has noted, enslavement sometimes followed the freed around (e.g., Nero's secretary, Epaphroditus). Furthermore, it is not as though when enslaved persons are manumitted, all the social and cultural and physical violence and oppression suddenly evaporate. Enslavement is not simply shed like a tunic. It haunts the lives and bodyminds of those who have experienced it. Many early Christian writers could have been and probably were freed people themselves. Would they not also provide an enslaved perspective on the ancient world? Should their literary texts, their letters, their treatises, not also count as enslaved literature? For how could a formerly enslaved person's thinking ever reset to a mode of creativity and intellectual ability that is devoid from the influence of an enslaved life? This notion challenges another default idea in our scholarship that we should presume Christian authors were freeborn unless there is evidence to the contrary. In a movement like early Christianity where there does seem to be some relative social mobility for enslaved people, how historically plausible is this?

Another point on intellectual ability is warranted. Even in cases where we are dealing with free Christian authors working with enslaved literary workers, to presume that the latter had no discernable influence on early Christian texts is also to presume a kind of limited intellectual stagnation, essentially carrying forward the caricature of literate workers as empty vessels through which the Author's ideas passed. Can ideas pass through a mind and not change the mind itself? Can words pass through a person and not shape their thinking? The incredible technical

---

[266] As Ella Grunberger-Kirsh has noted, we do have some first-hand accounts of writing from early Christian literate workers, such as Paulinus of Milan (*Life of Ambrose* 42) and Paul the Deacon (*Life of Gregory* I), 28. Grunberger-Kirsh, "Etched into the Soul," 69.

skill required to do sustained literary work, whether it be stenography, taking dictation, transcription, copying, and reading tells us that the workers with whom early Christian authors wrote were not intellectually limited. Is it likely that literate workers who worked with an author such as Origen, Augustine, or Jerome over long periods of time, perhaps even years, would not also improve in their own theological and intellectual capacities? Would they not have improved and grown in ability each time a new letter was written or a new treatise drafted? And would this compounding of ability not make them a valuable asset over time (provided their bodies allowed) in the creation of not only similar but new material? Most of all, do we think that ancient authors would not have taken advantage of the growing intellectual abilities of their literate workers despite already taking advantage of them as literary prostheses? As I see it, the hesitancy to attribute literary agency to ancient literate workers is influenced by the same simplistic and reductive caricature of the difference between a blue-collar and white-collar workers. There is a divide between the intellectual and the vocational. We are so sure that the named author, the intellectual, is primed with the capacity to write, to create, to *author*, while we are so frazzled by whether the literate worker, the vocational, is merely a mechanical instrument parroting the intellectual's genius. This not only reproduces a kind of modern classism, but also an implicit ableism. If we do not think that our ancient literary sources are truly authored and influenced by literate workers as well as their named authors, then we must subconsciously believe that literate workers had lower intellectual ability than their masters.

Someone might push back and argue that it is not that we think such literate workers had lower intellectual ability but that their masters exercised a dominating amount of control over what was written and what was eventually included. This may be overemphasizing a rhetorical trope in the ancient world, that masters not only claimed to have total control over written work but did so all the time. Jerome is an example of someone who claims to have had control but in reality as we saw in Section 5 did not. Additionally, this seems like special pleading from a practical perspective. If Jerome is dictating over three days thousands of lines of translation from Hebrew to Latin, which literate worker is there keeping track of all the ideas that Jerome comes up with and all the ideas that his literate workers come up with? Who keeps the tally? Furthermore, we have no objective data that tells us how much ancient writers expected literary work to originate only from their own minds. Some writers tell us they do lots of editing, others tell us that they do little. These may be the reality, or they may be an idealization. More importantly, given the fact that we have evidence of some authors who clearly acknowledge that their literate workers are prescient regarding the ideas in their heads and can write down the ideas before the words have been spoken – who, in these instances, should we classify as the author of the material? Ancient writers like Ausonius claim that it comes from his own mind, of course, but from a historical perspective we would say that if his literate worker writes down something that the named author had intended but had not yet communicated, that they, not the named author, created that idea. The stereotype of prescience betrays the influence of the literate workers in creating works that they scribed.

What is most problematic about presuming that ancient enslaved literate workers are invisible, that they are subsumed and untraceable in the literary works that they have created, that their enslaved experiences are not present in the early Christian archive we have is that this retains an enslaver's perspective on their work. If we are truly invested in recognizing the authorial and intellectual contributions of these enslaved workers to early Christian literature, then we must shed the last tendrils of these ideas. I am not saying that enslaved experiences and subjectivities ring clear *apart from named authors* in our sources. As Harriet Flower argues, the systems of enslavement in ancient world were designed to occlude the participation of even formerly enslaved literate persons: "Meanwhile, the traditional pattern of naming freedmen after their former masters can easily result in the elite Roman himself getting credit in later accounts for a work produced by someone he had formerly enslaved, a work that may have been conceived and written after the actual author's manumission."[267] The first step in hearing them is recognizing that they are there in the literary work that we have and that it is not necessarily the case that their voice is suppressed or dominated. Further analysis might show the latter to be true, but to presume the case is already to veil the potentiality latent in each literary work.

Critical fabulation *can* be a useful tool in for imagining the impossible, to bridge the gaps and lacunae in our ancient historical sources, especially related to enslavement and literate workers in the wider ancient Mediterranean, not least the development of early Christianity. The argument here is not that critical fabulation should not be used. We should be grateful for the pioneering work of scholars who are pressing the field forward by taking up new methodologies for seemingly intractable historiographical problems.

---

[267] Flower, "The Most Expensive Slave in Rome," 102.

Critical fabulation can be useful when we have a severely incomplete archive. But in the ancient world we have an enormous archive which many enslaved literate workers helped write and produce. The significance of the work of scholars like Moss is not only in opening up new vistas of insight into early Christian literary development or reorienting the field's understanding of an early Christian author. Many readers may not realize the extent to which her work has completely opened the door to enslaved literate workers in early Christian history.[268] But we do a disservice to the enslaved of the past by neglecting where they do speak by substituting it with our own speculative (even if informed) fabulations. As Trevor Burnard argues: "The methodological perspective that emphasizes the ways in which enslaved people were trapped within the tyranny of a restrictive archive thus underestimates enslaved people's capacity for agency."[269]

It is not simply that our sources *contain* traces of these workers inaccessible to us. That conception of ancient literature is predicated on the idea that named author and literate worker can be untethered from one another. Instead, our sources *are* the traces of the literate underclass. Although author and literate worker are indistinguishable from one another, the extant text is nevertheless a witness to the intellectual and physical abilities of the latter, just as they are a witness to the intellectual and physical abilities of the former. Each document is witness to the lived experience of (enslaved) literate workers, adulterated and mixed, to be sure, but lived experience, nonetheless. The unlearning that needs to happen is our own. We should absolutely go ahead and fabulate, but we should not do so at the expense of what is already available in the archive. As Joshel and Petersen argue, "There is...a thickness to slaves' lives that scholarship has yet to internalize."[270] Before we turn to imagination, we need to make sure first that we are not imaging the historical out of the archive itself. Because what is available, as I have argued in this Element, is greater than we realize.

---

[268] I am grateful to Katherine Huemoeller for reminding me of this important point.
[269] Burnard, *Writing the History of Global Slavery*, 56.
[270] Joshel and Petersen, *The Material Life of Roman Slaves*, 222.

Bibliography

Amidon, Philip R. trans. *Philostorgius: Church History*. Writings from the Greco-Roman World 23. Atlanta: Society of Biblical Literature, 2007.

Arns, Evaristo. *La technique du livre d'après sain Jérôme*. Paris: E. de Boccard, 1953.

Bakhos. "Orality and Writing." Pages 482–99 in *The Oxford Handbook of Jewish Daily Life in Roman Palestine*. Edited by Catherine Hezser. Oxford: Oxford University Press, 2010.

Blake, Sarah. "In Manus: Pliny's Letters and the Arts of Mastery." Pages 89–108 in *Roman Literary Cultures: Domestic Politics, Revolutionary Poetics, Civic Spectacle*. Edited by Alison Keith and Jonathan Edmonson. Toronto: University of Toronto Press, 2016.

Blake, Sarah. "Now You See Them: Slaves and Other Objects as Elements of the Roman Master." *Helios* 39 (2013): 193–211.

Bonar, Chance. "Notes." Pages 90–105 in *Writing, Enslavement, and Power in the Roman Mediterranean, 100 BCE–300 CE*. Edited by Jeremiah Coogan, Candida R. Moss, and Joseph A. Howley. Oxford: Oxford University Press, 2025.

Bonar, Chance. *The Author in Early Christian Literature*. Cambridge Elements. Cambridge: Cambridge University Press, 2025.

Brown, Vincent. "Social Death and Political Life in the Study of Slavery." *American Historical Review* 114 (2009): 1231–49.

Burnard, Trevor. *Writing the History of Global Slavery of Elements in Historical Theory and Practice*. Cambridge: Cambridge University Press, 2023.

Cain, Andrew. *Jerome's Commentaries on the Pauline Epistles and the Architecture of Exegetical Authority*. Oxford Early Christian Studies. Oxford: Oxford University Press, 2021.

Chin, Michael M. *Grammar and Christianity in the Late Roman World*. Philadelphia: University of Pennsylvania Press, 2007.

Coleman, Javal and Dan-el Padilla Peralta. "Rhetorics." Pages 232–51 in *Writing, Enslavement, and Power in the Roman Mediterranean, 100 BCE–300 CE*. Edited by Jeremiah Coogan, Candida R. Moss, and Joseph A. Howley. Oxford: Oxford University Press, 2025.

Coogan, Jeremiah, Candida R. Moss, and Joseph A. Howley. "Introduction." Pages 1–15 in *Writing, Enslavement, and Power in the Roman Mediterranean, 100 BCE–300 CE*. Edited by Jeremiah

Coogan, Candida R. Moss, and Joseph A. Howley. Oxford: Oxford University Press, 2025.

Coogan, Jeremiah. "Notes." Pages 156–66 in *Writing, Enslavement, and Power in the Roman Mediterranean, 100 BCE–300 CE*. Edited by Jeremiah Coogan, Candida R. Moss, and Joseph A. Howley. Oxford: Oxford University Press, 2025.

Coogan, Jeremiah. "Tabular Thinking in Late Ancient Palestine: Instrumentality, Work, and the Construction of Knowledge." Pages 57–82 in *Knowledge Construction in Late Antiquity*. Edited by Monika Amsler. Berlin: De Gruyter, 2023.

DeCock, Miriam. "Origen's Sources of Exegetical Authority: The Construction of an Inspired Exegete in the Pauline Lineage." *New Testament Studies* 70 (2024): 149–59.

Ehrman. *Forgery and Counter-Forgery: The Use of Literary Deceit in Early Christian Polemics.* Oxford: Oxford University Press, 2012.

Elder, Nicholas. *Gospel Medi: Reading, Writing, and Circulating Jesus Traditions.* Grand Rapids: Eerdmans, 2024.

Eno, Robert. *Saint Augustine. Letters.* Volume IV (1*–29*). Fathers of the Church 81. Washington, DC: The Catholic University of America Press, 1989.

Fitzgerald, Augustine. trans. *The Letters of Synesius of Cyrene.* London: Oxford University Press, 1926.

Flower, Harriet I. "The Most Expensive Slave in Rome: Quintus Lutatius Daphnis." *Classical Philology* 117 (2022): 99–119.

Garzya, Antonio, Denis Roques, and Synésios de Cyrène. *Correspondance. Lettres I-LXIII.* Paris: Belles lettres, 2000.

Glancy, Jennifer. *Slavery in Early Christianity*. Oxford: Oxford University Press, 2002.

Goodman, Martin. "Text, Scribes and Power in Roman Judea." Pages 79–90 in *Judaism in the Roman World*. Ancient Judaism and Early Christianity 66. Leiden: Brill, 2007.

Graumann, Thomas. *The Acts of the Early Church Councils: Production and Character.* Oxford Early Christian Studies. Oxford: Oxford University Press, 2021.

Graves, Michael. *Jerome's Hebrew Philology: A Study Based on His Commentary on Jeremiah*. VCSup. 90. Leiden: Brill, 2007.

Grunberger-Kirsh, Ella. "'Etched into the Soul': The Education of Shorthand-Writers in Late Antiquity." *Journal of Roman Studies* 114 (2024): 61–84.

Habinek, Thomas. "Slavery and Class." Pages 385–93 in *A Companion to Latin Literature*. Edited by Stephen Harrison. London: Blackwell, 2005.

Hagendahl, Harald. "Die Bedeutung der Stenographie für die spätlateinische christliche Literatur." *Jahrbuch für Antike und Christentum* 14 (1971): 24–38.

Haines-Eitzen, Kim. "Girls Trained in Beautiful Writing': Female Scribes in Roman Antiquity and Early Christianity." *Journal of Early Christian Studies* 6 (1998): 629–46.

Haines-Eitzen, Kim. *Guardians of Letters: Literacy, Power, and the Transmitters of Early Christian Literature*. Oxford: Oxford University Press, 2000.

Haines-Eitzen, Kim. "The Social History of Early Christian Scribes." Pages 479–95 in *The Text of the New Testament in Contemporary Research: Essays on the Status Quaestionis*. Edited by Bart D. Ehrman and Michael W. Holmes. Second Edition. New Testament Tools, Studies and Documents 42. Leiden: Brill, 2013.

Hartman, Saidiya. "Venus in Two Acts." *Small Axe* 12 (2008): 1–14.

Havelková, Brukner, et al. "Ancient Egyptian Scribes and Specific Skeletal Occupational Risk Markers (Abusir, Old Kingdom)." *Scientific Reports* 14, 13317 (2024): 1–19.

Head, Peter M. "Named Letter-Carriers among the Oxyrhynchus Papyri." *Journal for the Study of the New Testament* 31 (2009): 279–99.

Heine, Ronald E. *The Commentary of Origen on the Gospel of St. Matthew*. Oxford Early Christian Texts. Oxford: Oxford University Press, 2018.

Hezser, Catherine. *Jewish Literacy in Roman Palestine*. Texts and Studies in Ancient Judaism 81. Tübingen: Mohr Siebeck, 2001.

Horsfall, Nicholas. "Rome without Spectacles." *Greece & Rome* 42 (1995): 49–56.

Houghton, H. A. G. "The Fourth Century and the Beginning of the Vulgate." Pages 19–42 in *The Latin New Testament: A Guide to Its Early History, Texts, and Manuscripts*. Oxford: Oxford University Press, 2016.

Howley, Joseph. *Aulus Gellius and Roman Reading Culture: Text, Presence, and Imperial Knowledge*. Cambridge: Cambridge University Press, 2018.

Howley, Joseph. "Despotics." Pages 24–43 in *Writing, Enslavement, and Power in the Roman Mediterranean, 100 BCE–300 CE*. Eds. Jeremiah Coogan, Candida R. Moss, and Joseph A. Howley. Oxford: Oxford University Press, 2025.

Howley, Joseph. "Intellectual Narratives and Elite Roman Learning in the 'Noctes Atticae' of Aulus Gellius." PhD Dissertation. St. Andrews University, 2011.

Howley, Joseph. "Reading in Ancient Rome." Pages 15–27 in *Further Reading*. Edited by Matthew Rubery and Leah Price. Oxford: Oxford University Press, 2020.

Huemoeller, Katherine. "Lost and (Not) Found: An Enslaved Woman's Voice in Plutarch's Life of Crassus." *Classical Philology* (forthcoming).

Johnson, William A. *Readers and Reading Cultures in the High Roman Empire: A Study of Elite Communities*. Classical Culture and Society. Oxford: Oxford University Press, 2010.

Joshel, Sandra R. and Lauren Hackworth Petersen. *The Material Life of Roman Slaves*. Cambridge: Cambridge University Press, 2014.

Kearey, Talitha. "Editing." Pages 186–204 in *Writing, Enslavement, and Power in the Roman Mediterranean, 100 BCE–300 CE*. Edited by Jeremiah Coogan, Candida R. Moss, and Joseph A. Howley. Oxford: Oxford University Press, 2025.

Kloeters, Gert. "Buch und Schrift bei Heronymus." PhD Dissertation. Münster, 1957.

Lambert, Cat. "Gender." Pages 44–59 in *Writing, Enslavement, and Power in the Roman Mediterranean, 100 BCE–300 CE*. Edited by Jeremiah Coogan, Candida R. Moss, and Joseph A. Howley. Oxford: Oxford University Press, 2025.

Lapin, Hayim. *Rabbis as Romans: The Rabbinic Movement in Palestine, 100–400 CE*. Oxford: Oxford University Press, 2012.

Mcdonnell, Myles. "Writing, Copying, and Autograph Manuscripts in Ancient Rome." *The Classical Quarterly* 46 (1996): 469–91.

McKeown, Niall. *The Invention of Ancient Slavery? Duckworth Classical Essays*. London: Duckworth, 2007.

Metzger, Bruce M. *Historical and Literary Studies: Pagan, Jewish, and Christian*. New Testament Tools, Studies and Documents 8. Leiden: Brill, 1968.

Meyer, Elizabeth. "Roman Tabulae, Egyptian Christians, and the Adoption of the Codex." *Chiron. Mitteilungen der Kommission für Alte Geschichte und Epigraphik des Deutschen Archäologischen Instituts* 37 (2007): 295–348.

Moss, Candida. "Disability." Pages 60–70 in *Writing, Enslavement, and Power in the Roman Mediterranean, 100 BCE–300 CE*. Edited by

Jeremiah Coogan, Candida R. Moss, and Joseph A. Howley. Oxford: Oxford University Press, 2025.

Moss, Candida. "Fashioning Mark: Early Christian Discussions about the Scribe and Status of the Second Gospel." *New Testament Studies* 67 (2021): 181–204.

Moss, Candida. *God's Ghostwriters: Enslaved Christians and the Making of the Bible*. New York City: Little, Brown, and Company, 2024.

Moss, Candida. "The Secretary: What Large Letters: Enslaved Workers, Stenography, and the Production of Early Christian Literature." *The Journal of Theological Studies* 74 (2023): 20–56.

Nobbs, Alanna M. "Philostorgius' Ecclesiastical History: An 'Alternative Ideology'." *Tyndale Bulletin* 42 (1991): 271–81.

Nongbri, Brent. February 4, 2025. "A Mosaic from Thabraca with a Writer at a Desk." Variant Readings. https://brentnongbri.com/2025/02/05/a-mosaic-from-thabraca-with-a-writer-at-a-desk/

Nongbri, Brent. August 11, 2024. "A Relief from Ostia Showing Writers at Desks." Variant Readings. https://brentnongbri.com/2024/08/11/a-relief-from-ostia-showing-writers-at-desks/

Nongbri, Brent. August 13, 2024. "A Relief from Portus Showing a Writer at a Desk." Variant Readings. https://brentnongbri.com/2024/08/13/a-relief-from-portus-showing-a-writer-at-a-desk/

Nongbri, Brent. "Maintenance." Pages 167–85 in *Writing, Enslavement, and Power in the Roman Mediterranean, 100 BCE–300 CE*. Edited by Jeremiah Coogan, Candida R. Moss, and Joseph A. Howley. Oxford: Oxford University Press, 2025.

Nongbri, Brent. March 8, 2025. "The So-called Scriptorium at Bu Njem." Variant Readings. https://brentnongbri.com/2025/03/08/the-so-called-scriptorium-at-bu-njem/

Norden, Eduard. *Die antike Kuntsprosa vom VI. Jahrhundert v. Chrs. bis in die Zeit der Renaissance*. Band II. Berlin: Teubner, 1995.

Ommundsen, Å., et al. "How Many Medieval and Early Modern Manuscripts Were Copied by Female Scribes? A Bibliometric Analysis Based on Colophons." *Humanities and Social Science Communications* 12 (2025): 346.

Preuschen, Erwin. "Die Stenographie im Leben des Origenes." *Archiv für Stenographie* 56 (1905): 6–15, 49–55.

Price, Richard and Michael Gaddis, trans. *The Acts of the Council of Chalcedon*. Volume Two. Translated Texts for Historians 45. Liverpool: Liverpool University Press, 2005.

Ratkus, Artūras. "Greek ἀρχιερεύς in Gothic Translation." *Nowele* 71 (2018): 3–34.

Reay, Brendon. "Agriculture, Writing, and Cato's Aristocratic Self-Fashioning." *Classical Antiquity* 24 (2005): 331–61.

Richlin, Amy. *Slave Theater in the Roman Republic: Plautus and Popular Comedy.* Cambridge: Cambridge University Press, 2017.

Schams, Christine. *Jewish Scribes in the Second-Temple Perio.* JSOTSup 291. Sheffield: Sheffield Academic Press, 1998.

Schlumberger, Jörg. "'Non scribo sed dicto': (HA, T 33,8). Hat der Autor der Historia Augusta mit Stenographen gearbeitet?" Pages 221–38 in *Bonner Historia-Augusta-Colloquium 1972/1974.* Antiquitas, Reihe 4, Beiträge zur Historia-Augusta-Forschung. Bonn: Rudolf Habelt Verlag, 1976.

Schultz, Alexandra Leewon. "Collection." Pages 205–24 in *Writing, Enslavement, and Power in the Roman Mediterranean, 100 BCE–300 CE.* Edited by Jeremiah Coogan, Candida R. Moss, and Joseph A. Howley. Oxford: Oxford University Press, 2025.

Shaner, Katherine. *Enslaved Leadership in Early Christianity.* Oxford: Oxford University Press, 2018.

Skeat, T. C. "Early Christian Book-Production: Papyri and Manuscripts." Pages 54–79 in *The Cambridge History of the Bible.* Edited by G. W. H. Lampe. *The Cambridge History of The Bible.* Cambridge: Cambridge University Press, 1969.

Skeat, T. C. "The Use of Dictation in Ancient Book Production." Pages 1–32 in *The Collected Biblical Writings of T.C. Skeat.* Edited by J. K. Elliot. *NovTSup 113.* Leiden: Brill, 2004.

Soon, Isaac. *A Disabled Apostle: Impairment and Disability in the Letters of Paul.* Oxford: Oxford University Press, 2023.

Soon, Isaac. "The Alexamenos Graffito as Christian Self-Parody." New Testament Studies (forthcoming).

Starr, Raymond J. "The Circulation of Literary Texts in the Roman World." *The Classical Quarterly* 37 (1987): 213–23.

Teilter, Hans. *Notarii and exceptores: An Inquiry into Role and Significance of notarii and exceptores in the Imperial and Ecclesiastical Bureaucracy of the Roman Empire (from the Early Principate to circa 450 A.D.).* Dutch Monographs on Ancient History and Archaeology 1. Amsterdam: Gieben, 1985.

Tempest, Kathryn. "Tiro, Marcus Tullius." Pages 6764–67 in *The Encyclopedia of Ancient History*, First Edition. Edited by Roger S. Bagnall et al. London: Blackwell, 2013.

Tomlin, Roger S. O. *Roman London's First Voices: Writing Tablets from the Bloomberg Excavations, 2010–14*. Museum of London Archaeology Monograph 72. London: Museum of London Archaeology, 2016.

Tupamahu, Ekaputra. "Language and Ethnicity." Pages 71–83 in *Writing, Enslavement, and Power in the Roman Mediterranean, 100 BCE–300 CE*. Edited by Jeremiah Coogan, Candida R. Moss, and Joseph A. Howley. Oxford: Oxford University Press, 2025.

Vlassopoulos, Kostas. *Historicizing Ancient Slavery*. Edinburgh Studies in Ancient Slavery. Edinburgh: Edinburgh University Press, 2023.

Wise, Michael Owen. *Language and Literacy in Roman Judea: A Study of the Bar Kokhba Documents*. Anchor Bible Yale Reference Library. New Haven: Yale University Press, 2015.

Yadin, Yigael J., et al., *Documents from the Bar Kokhba Period in the Cave of the Letters*, Vol. 3. Hebrew, Aramaic and Nabatean-Aramaic Papyri. Jerusalem: Israel Exploration Society, 2002.

Cambridge Elements⁼

Early Christian Literature

Garrick V. Allen
University of Glasgow
Garrick V. Allen (PhD St Andrews, 2015) is Professor of Divinity and Biblical Criticism at the University of Glasgow. He is the author of multiple articles and books on the New Testament, early Jewish and Christian literature, and ancient and medieval manuscript traditions, including *Manuscripts of the Book of Revelation: New Philology, Paratexts, Reception* (Oxford University Press, 2020) and *Words are Not Enough: Paratexts, Manuscripts, and the Real New Tesatament* (Eerdmans, 2024). He is the winner of the Manfred Lautenschlaeger Award for Theological Promise and the Paul J. Achetemeier Award for New Testament Scholarship.

About the Series
This series sets new research agendas for understanding early Christian literature, exploring the diversity of Christian literary practices through the contexts of ancient literary production, the forms of literature composed by early Christians, themes related to particular authors, and the languages in which these works were written.

Cambridge Elements

Early Christian Literature

Elements in the Series

The Author in Early Christian Literature
Chance E. Bonar

Maximos the Confessor: Androprimacy and Sexual Difference
Luis Josué Salés

Egeria: Theological and Ecclesial Knowledge Between Eastern and Western Traditions
Anni Maria Laato

The Pseudo-Clementine *Tradition: The Hermeneutics of Late-Ancient Sophistic Christianity*
Benjamin M. J. De Vos

Literate Workers and the Production of Early Christian Literature
Isaac T. Soon

A full series listing is available at: www.cambridge.org/EECL

Printed by Integrated Books International,
United States of America